DIY BEDROOM DÉCOR

50 Awesome IDEAS for Your Room

Tana Smith

A adamsmedia

Avon, Massachusetts

Published by
Adams Media, a division of F+W Media, Inc.
57 Littlefield Street, Avon, MA 02322. U.S.A.
www.adamsmedia.com

ISBN 10: 1-4405-8802-3
ISBN 13: 978-1-4405-8802-0
eISBN 10: 1-4405-8803-1
eISBN 13: 978-1-4405-8803-7

Printed by R.R. Donnelley Asia, Shenzhen, China.
10 9 8 7 6 5 4 3 2 1
April 2015

Cover design by Frank Rivera.
Cover images © Debby Wolvos.
Step-by-step photography and materials photography by Tana Smith.
All other photography by Debby Wolvos.

This book is available at quantity discounts for bulk purchases.
For information, please call 1-800-289-0963.

I would like to dedicate this book to:

All of my YouTube subscribers, whom I consider my friends and biggest supporters. I want to thank you all for encouraging me to pursue a love that I didn't even know I had.

To my family, for being interested and supportive in this process. Especially my #1 fan, my mom. Thanks for giving me the courage to accept any challenge, and to never admit defeat.

A special thanks to my boyfriend Philippe, for putting up with the madwoman tasked with writing a book in two months, through glue gun burns and shoots lasting until 3 A.M. This never would have been possible without all of your support.

CONTENTS

INTRODUCTION

Do you want to revamp a boring bedroom? Bring your personal style into your space? Make sure everyone who goes into your room knows exactly who you are and what you like? Well, whether you want to amp up your space with glitter, paint, fabric, or lighting, you're in the right place!

The fifty projects found throughout *DIY Bedroom Décor* give you a super-fun way to express yourself that you won't find anywhere else! Make your room sparkle with projects like the Sequin Heart, Gold Pillowcase, or Glitter-Dipped Feather Garland; shine with Ping-Pong Ball Lights or a Ribbon Chandelier; or just showcase who you are with a Lighted Floral Peace Sign, Antler Jewelry Holder, or Sunburst Mirror. These fun and easy DIY projects give you so many cute ways to decorate your room, all of which are much less expensive and much more personal than just buying something generic at the store.

In addition, throughout the book you'll learn how to take the ideas that are presented in these projects and customize them, expand on them, and make your own truly unique decorations! This idea represents the best part of DIY projects—the idea that you truly get to think out a project by yourself, prep it by yourself, and bring it into reality by yourself!

So get your crafting tools ready, grab all of your materials, and get inspired to make over your bedroom with these awesome, on-trend DIY projects!

CRAFT SUPPLIES TO HAVE ON HAND

The world of DIY is enormous, but it doesn't have to be overwhelming! If you're not sure what you should have on hand, this chapter will steer you in the right direction, mapping out key tools to guide you along your way—even if you have no idea where to start! The craft store will become your new best friend as you search for everything you'll need to take your room from flat to fancy, so stock up on the basics *before* you start on your bedroom transformation to make the DIY projects you find in this book that much easier!

Glue Gun

A glue gun is a crafter's best friend. It is a versatile tool that can bring together even the most stubborn pieces of crafting material. Always use caution when working with a glue gun since the tip gets very hot, and remember to prop your glue gun up correctly to prevent the hot tip from touching anything that it shouldn't.

Scissors

Many of the projects in this book call for scissors. You probably have a pair of scissors in your house already, but not all scissors are created equal. Scissors should be able to make clean cuts in many different types of materials. You don't want to use scissors that will tear, rip, break, or fray your materials. If you want your cuts to come out crisp, make sure that your scissors are not dull. If you need to determine whether your scissors are sharp enough to make great DIY crafts, all you need to do is use your scissors to cut some construction paper. If the scissors cut through the paper crisply and leave a nice edge, then you are good to go. If the paper ends up with frayed edges or does not come apart cleanly, you should replace them with a pair of new, sharp scissors. It seems like such a simple thing, but it can make a big difference in how your projects turn out.

Utility Knife

A utility knife, such as an X-Acto, can be a very useful alternative to scissors when you want extra precision or need to cut against a flat surface. Utility knives are commonly found in craft stores so it should be easy to find one when you are searching for your other materials. While using a utility knife you should always have a surface you don't mind getting scratched and cut below the material your are cutting. Cardboard is a good option, but anything that is hard and you don't mind getting beat up will work.

Paintbrushes

When it comes to applying paint, there are many different types of brushes you can use, such as a sponge brush or synthetic-bristle paintbrush. For the projects in this book, the type of paintbrush you use will not make a huge difference. That said, consider using a sponge brush when applying paint to large objects. Sponge brushes are easy to use and cost less than traditional paintbrushes, which makes them ideal for DIY projects. They come in all sizes, but the 1" size will be perfect for all of the projects that use them in this book. Sponge brushes are great for quickly adding a thick wash of paint to whatever project you are working on.

A synthetic-bristle paintbrush can be used the same way, but the application will most likely require a few coats. Look for a brush with bristles that are ½" to 1" wide, so you can use it for more precise application when working on detailed projects.

Mod Podge

No craft arsenal is complete without Mod Podge, an all-purpose gluing material that can be used in many different ways while you're crafting. Use it to add a finishing coat to a project, as a sticky base to add glitter to, or even to stick things together. Mod Podge is easily found at nearly any craft store, as well as at online retailers like Amazon. While there are many varieties to choose from, glossy Mod Podge is the best for what you're going to be doing here. It's great to have on hand, and will help you complete many of the projects in this book.

So now that you are armed with the basic tools to make crafting a breeze, get ready to transform your room with *DIY Bedroom Décor*!

CH1

WALL
ART

One of the simplest ways to dress up your room is by adding lots of fun and trendy decorations to your walls. It's so much fun to decorate, and what could be better than dressing up your walls with stuff that you have made yourself? Wall art is the bread and butter of room decoration, and you don't have to settle for store-bought items that everyone else already has. In this chapter, you will find ideas for dressing up your walls with unique décor that includes everything from a Framed Fabric Bulletin Board to a Marquee Sign to an Ombré Painted Canvas. Everything you'll learn how to make in this chapter is super affordable, so you won't be limited in what you can create. Pick a few projects, five, or even more! Once you get on a roll, you won't want to stop. With these awesome wall art projects, you'll be on your way to having that super-cool room you've always dreamed of!

GOLD FOIL PRINTS

Prints can be so expensive, but making your own is half the cost and twice the fun! For your print, think about using the first letter of your name, a perfume bottle, or even a yummy cupcake. Anything goes! You can freehand your own design, or create your own stencil by printing cool images from the Internet. Just add the word "silhouette" at the end of your Internet searches to ensure your print comes out looking fabulously clear every time. The Gold Foil Prints will look great hanging on that boring wall above your bed, or propped up on your nightstand. The gold pop is exactly what you need to make your room look chic and super fun.

materials

- Shape silhouette printed on 8" × 10" printer paper
- Utility knife (such as an X-Acto)
- 1 (8" × 10") photo frame
- 3 (11" × 14") sheets card stock or posterboard
- Gold gilding paint
- 1 (1") sponge brush

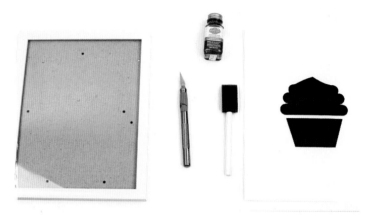

①

1 Use your utility knife to cut along the outside border of the black shape you printed, to create a stencil. Do this for as many prints as you want to make.

Make It Personal!

Hanging these in a horizontal line of three is the best way to display your creation and catch people's attention. However, these gold foil prints will look just as great on their own propped up on your nightstand.

2 Using the cardboard insert from your photo frame as a guide, cut your card stock with the utility knife so it fits into your picture frame.

3 Center the stencil over the card stock and use the sponge brush to apply the gilding paint. Begin by pressing the sides of the stencil down as you paint inward along the edges in small sections, to make sure that no paint gets underneath the stencil. Then, once you have the gold outline, fill in the rest of the space inside the shape with the paint to complete the design.

4 When the gilding paint is dry (check the recommended drying time on the bottle), remove the stencil and place the print into the frame. Then put the frame back together and display it in your room.

FRAME WALL

chapter 1 *mom*

Frame walls look best when you use frames of different sizes, shapes, and colors, so don't be afraid to step out of the box with this DIY project. There is no wrong way to do this! You can make this project super personal by printing out all of your favorite pictures and popping them into frames. Or, if you don't want to use photos, this project works great with scrapbook paper or magazine cutouts. This is such an easy way to turn the things you love into art for your room. The possibilities really are endless!

materials

- 4 or more assorted photo frames, different shapes and colors
- 4 or more printed pictures/scrapbook paper/magazine cutouts/printed quotes (1 per frame, sized for the frame it will go in)
- Scissors
- 4 or more nails or pushpins (optional)

1 Take the picture frames you've chosen to use for this project and arrange them into a cluster on the floor. Feel free to rearrange and mix them up until you have a pattern you like. An easy way to figure out how to arrange your frames is to start by lining your frames up into equal two rows. Then, adjust two of the frames so they are slightly off center. Using frames of different shapes and sizes makes your frame wall fun to look at. You can even position half of the frames vertically and the other half horizontally.

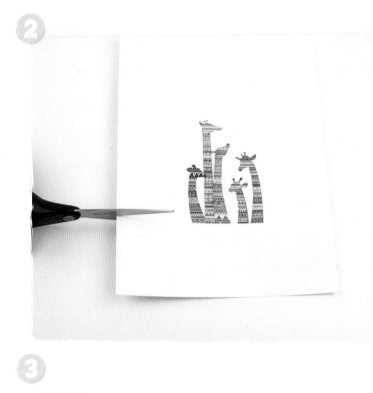

2 Take your printed photos and decide which frames you want to put them in. Then, one at a time, open up your picture frame and cut your printed photo to fit, using the cardboard photo insert that comes with the frame as your guide.

3 Once your picture is the correct size, place it in the corresponding frame. Repeat for the other pictures and frames. Finally, hang each frame one at a time using nails or pushpins and the hanging hooks on the back of each frame if desired, transferring the layout you created on your floor onto the wall.

FRAMED FABRIC
BULLETIN BOARD

Bulletin boards are an essential for any girl's desk. They're awesome for displaying A+ grades, love notes from your crush, or reminding you about Friday night FroYo with the girls. But why settle for a generic corkboard when you can make something that's totally your own? Have fun picking adorable fabric to match your room décor for the ultimate personal touch.

materials

- 1 (11" × 14") ornate wooden frame found at a craft store
- Acrylic paint (any color of your choice)
- 1 (1") sponge brush
- Cork roll (you'll need this to be just slightly larger than the interior dimensions of your frame, so make sure you have enough in the roll and that it's wide enough)
- Scissors
- 1 yard cotton fabric
- Glue gun
- Mounting tape (or hanger of your choice)

1 Start by painting the entire front of your frame with your sponge brush. You may need two coats to make the color opaque. Set aside to dry.

Make It Yours!

I used cotton fabric for this project because I like the pattern that it had, but if you find another material with a pattern you like, go ahead and use it!

2 Once the frame is dry, flip it over so the unpainted side is facing up. Then, take your cork roll and measure out then cut a piece that is 12" × 15". You want the cork to be a bit larger than the inside border of your frame. Leaving a little extra cork will allow you to attach it to the back of your frame later

3 Next, cut your fabric to be 16" × 13". When cutting the fabric, make sure that the fabric is bigger than the cork piece on all sides.

4 You are now ready to glue your fabric to the cork roll. Do this by making a large X in the middle of the cork with glue, then pressing the fabric down over the cork. Make sure the fabric is secure along the sides by lining the edges with glue as well. For the inch of excess fabric you left on all sides, pull it to the back of the cork and glue down so the rough edges aren't visible from the front. You should be left with a piece of cork that is tightly wrapped in fabric.

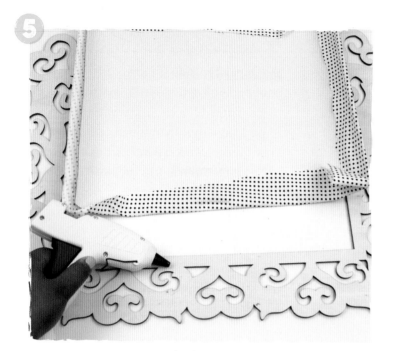

5 Now, with your frame still face down, glue the fabric-wrapped cork to the frame by lining the frame's outermost edges with glue, then pressing down firmly on the cork to secure. The fabric-covered side of the cork should face out of the frame.

6 Let your creation dry for about 30 minutes. Hang with mounting tape and enjoy!

HEART-SHAPED PICTURE COLLAGE

This project is the ultimate way to personalize your room, and it only takes a few minutes. Gather pictures of you and your friends and family throughout the years—yes, even those ones from your mortifying days of wearing braces! Memories with friends and family are nice to look at, and arranging them into a heart on your wall guarantees that your room is 100 percent on trend. If you need more pictures, mix in ones that you find online to fill in what you don't have. Just resize them to the standard 4" × 6" size, and you'll be feeling the love from this Heart-Shaped Picture Collage in no time!

materials

- 41 (4" × 6") printed photos
- Double-sided tape

1 Rows 1–2: Use the double-sided tape to attach a photo to the wall in the place where you want the bottom point of the heart to be. This will be the basis for the entire heart, so put it in a spot where you have enough room on both sides as well as above to create the heart. Directly above the first row, tape two pictures side by side, leaving a small space between the pictures.

2 Rows 3–5: Directly above the second row, tape four pictures side by side, leaving a small space between the pictures. Complete rows 4 through 5 in the exact same way, adding an additional picture as you

move up to each new row. As you work, be sure to keep the spacing as even as possible; the goal is to have the heart shape be even. If any of the rows seem like they are too wide, adjust the spacing to make the row fit better into the heart shape.

3 Row 6: As you did for row 5, tape six photos side by side, but this time adjust the spacing to be slightly bigger than that of the previous rows so that it extends out to the sides further than row 5, even though you're using the same amount of pictures.

4 Row 7: For this row, take seven pictures and tape them to the wall, leaving a small space between them as you did in rows 3–5. This will be the longest row.

5 Row 8: Take six pictures and divide them up into two groups of three. Center three pictures over each side, leaving a large space in the middle. This will begin to create the two sides of the heart.

6 Row 9: For this last row, take four photos and divide them up into groups of two. Place two photos over each grouping of three you did in row 8 to finish the heart shape.

PAINTED STICKER WALL DECAL

Today, wall decals are all the rage, and making your own wall decals is easier than you think! All you need to complete this project are stickers, paint, and a lazy afternoon. Decals are a fun and simple way to customize your room, and everyone who sees them is sure to be impressed! Wall decals are especially awesome because you can change them up whenever you get bored, so get creative with different designs and shapes, a super-cool geometric pattern, or a flock of birds flying by. The sky's the limit!

materials

- At least 30 jumbo stickers (each roughly 1"–4")
- 1–3 (2-ounce) bottles acrylic paint (depending on how large your stickers are)
- 1 (½") sponge brush

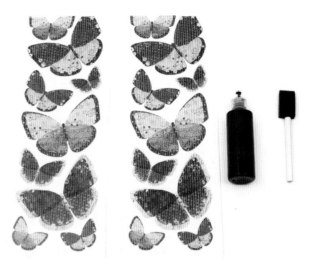

1 To begin, gently paint over the sticker sheet in long strokes, using a sponge brush so the sticker doesn't lift from its backing. Be sure to leave the stickers stuck to their backing until the last step to make painting the stickers easier and less messy.

2 You may need more than one coat of paint, depending on the color and design on your stickers. Just remember to let them dry for 10 minutes or so between coats.

3 When you are satisfied with the color, let your creation dry to the touch; this should take about 1 hour. Once dry, remove the stickers from their backings and place them in a design on the wall.

4 To make the wall design seen in the photos, stick the butterflies to the wall in a small circle, leaving the center open. Continue to add more butterflies to the outside of the first circle, orienting the butterflies so it looks like they are flying outward. You can continue to make the circle wider by adding more butterflies. As the circles get bigger, the butterflies should be spaced further away from each other. As you work, take a few steps back to make sure the placement looks good from far away. Since these are stickers, they are very easy to remove and replace in different spots, so it's okay if you mess up; just remove and place them again! Keep working outward until you are satisfied with the size.

Make It Personal!

To make your custom decals, choose a sticker with a smooth surface that you like the shape of. Since you'll be painting the stickers, the pattern or color doesn't matter too much. I chose butterflies for my decal in three sticker sizes: 4", 2", and 1". The smallest sticker you use should be around 1"; try to aim for a larger size, around 4", for the majority of your stickers. You will need at least 30 stickers to make a medium-sized wall design.

GLITTER STATE CANVAS

This is a great project for all you glitter lovers out there! Gather up a few of your friends and represent your state by making it shine with this totally cool Glitter State Canvas. You can do this with your home state, the state you've always dreamed of visiting, or both! And don't worry, making a stencil for this project is so easy. Just print out your state's outline, and it's all smooth sailing from there. So get ready to make your state shine! Ready, set, *glitter*!

materials

Stencil

- 1 (8" × 10") sheet of computer paper
- Scissors

Glitter State Canvas

- 1 (12" × 9") canvas
- State stencil
- Scotch tape
- 1 (1") sponge brush
- Mod Podge
- Glitter
- Paper towel (optional)

1 To make the stencil: Start by searching online for an outline of the state you want to create on canvas. You want to make sure that it will fill most of your canvas, so before you print, resize the state so that it will fill most of your 8" × 10" sheet of printer paper. I resized mine to 7" × 9" for a perfect fit.

2 To create the stencil, make a slight fold in the middle of the paper and cut into the fold slightly to start it off. From the middle of the paper, cut around the state outline leaving only the white, nonprinted outside of the paper intact. You will then be left with just the outline of your state. Keep this; it's your stencil!

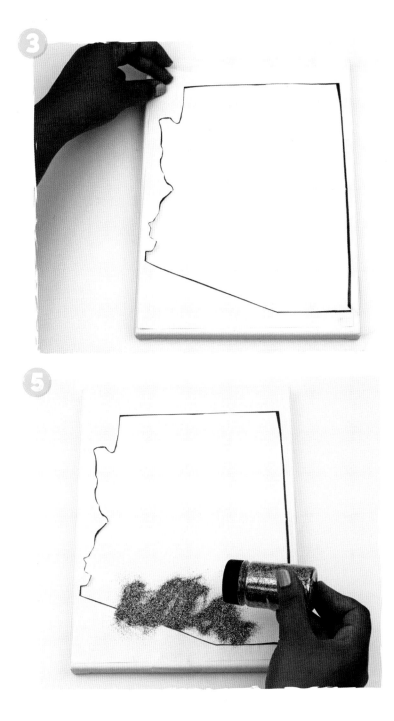

3 To make the Glitter State Canvas: Now, use the Scotch tape to secure your stencil to the canvas so it does not move while you work.

4 Use a sponge brush to apply a thin layer of Mod Podge to a small portion of the inside of the stencil. It's best to paint around the borders of the state first and work your way in toward the middle. Do not apply too large of a section at a time, as the Mod Podge dries fast.

5 Pour a layer of glitter over the Mod Podge you just applied. Try to get a thick coating of glitter to ensure you aren't left with empty spots. Pour any excess glitter off onto a paper plate so that you can use it again.

6 Continue adding Mod Podge, then glitter, until the entire state is filled, then let it sit to dry for about 15 minutes. Carefully remove the stencil and clean up the edges of your state using a paper towel to wipe away any glitter and Mod Podge that went outside the lines.

7 Now, use the sponge brush to apply a second layer of Mod Podge over the glitter state to lock everything in. Wait for the Mod Podge to completely dry, about 30 minutes, then hang your glitter state canvas up and show your pride!

MARQUEE SIGN

Catch a bit of the Hollywood glamour by making your very own Marquee Sign. These signs are super popular, but buying one can get pretty pricey. The great thing about making your own is that you are not limited to what is sold in stores. Just take a few cardboard letters, some paint, and add a string of round lights for the ultimate room decoration. If you want to get fancy, grab a cardboard star, paint it gold, and add the lights to create an awesome twist on this favorite. Be creative!

materials

- Hollow cardboard letters
- Utility knife (such as an X-Acto)
- Acrylic paint
- 1 (1") sponge brush
- Pencil
- Ruler
- 1 strand round-bulbed string lights (this is enough to create a three-letter word, with about 10 lights per letter)
- 2 thumbtacks per letter (optional)

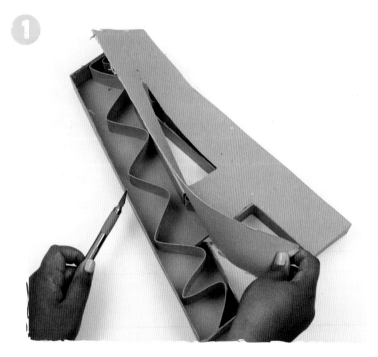

1 Start by using your utility knife to cut the front of the cardboard letter off. Insert the knife tip into the side of the letter, as close to the front edge as you can without going over the edge to the front itself, and cut. Once the entire front of the letter is open, remove the inner lining from the cardboard letter.

2 Next, apply a coat of paint to the inside of each letter. You may need to use two coats of paint to make sure your cardboard is all one color. Set aside to dry for about 1 hour. (See following photo.)

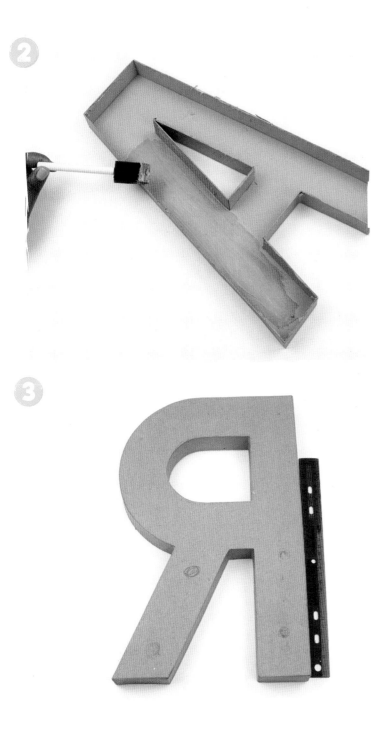

3 Once the paint is dry, sketch out where you want your lights to go by using your pencil to make a circle on the back of the letter where each light will be placed. The circles should be about the size of the bulbs on your string of lights, and equally spaced apart. You will use about 10 lights per letter, so you should have 10 circles. Use your ruler to make sure the circles are evenly spaced. A good rule of thumb is to place them 4" apart, though this may vary with the size of your letters and the number of lights you have. These circles will give you a rough idea of where each light will go.

4 Repeat the previous steps for each additional letter you'll use in your sign.

5 Next, lay out your word painted side down with the letters in reverse order, so that it reads from right to left. Use your utility knife to create X-shaped cuts in the center of each circle you sketched on the cardboard. These holes should be big enough to fit the socket of the light through, but not so large that the bulb will fit through. (See following photo.)

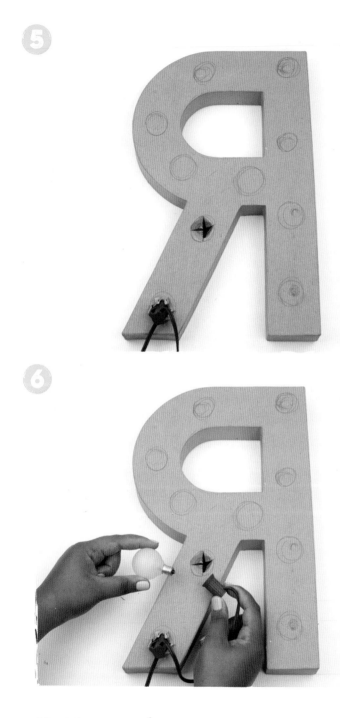

6 Remove the bulb from the first light and push the socket through the hole you made. Once the socket is through the hole, lift up the letter and screw the bulb back on from the front side to secure it. Unless the letter you are making is straight up and down, like an "L", while looking at the back-side of the letter, you want to start adding your lights at the bottom right of the first letter in the word, go up and around the letter, and end at the bottom left of each letter. This will make it easier when switching to the next letter, since you're using the same strand of lights.

7 Once the lights are fastened on each letter, your Marquee Sign is complete. If desired, use thumbtacks to hang it up on your wall near an electric outlet so you can plug it in.

Make It Personal!

To make this project a little easier, just use the Ping-Pong Ball Lights from Chapter 6. Simply wait until you poke the lights through the cardboard let-ters to attach the Ping-Pong balls to the bulbs.

BRANDY MELVILLE–STYLE DOOR SIGN

Brandy Melville signs are so popular right now that you've probably seen them somewhere! Fortunately, these painted signs with quotes on them are super easy to make. All you need is some paint, letter stickers, and a bit of wood, and you can be trendy too!

materials

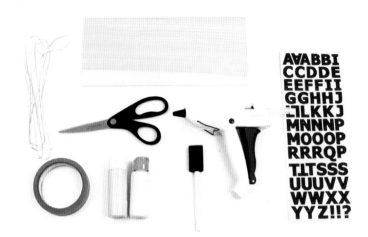

- 1 (5¼" × 12") piece pine craft wood (available at your local craft store)
- 2 shades acrylic paint
- 2 (1") sponge brushes
- 1 roll ¾"–1" painter's tape
- Glitter letter stickers (½") (the number of stickers needed depends on the number of letters in your quote)
- 6" 12-gauge craft wire (optional)
- Glue gun

1

1 Use your sponge brush to paint your entire wood plank with the first color you chose, then put aside to dry for about 30 minutes. The letters and border on your sign will end up being this color later, so keep that in mind when choosing. I chose white paint to be the color for my letters.

2 Once the paint has dried completely, apply painter's tape around the edges of the plank, keeping half of the tape visible on the front and folding the other half around the edge to the back.

3 Arrange your glitter letter stickers to form your quote on the middle section of the wood. When you like the placement, peel the stickers off the backing and make sure they are pressed down securely. Using glitter stickers in this step will make it easier to peel them off once you paint over them in the next step.

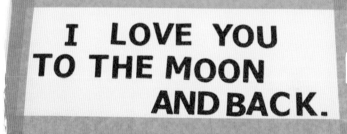

I LOVE YOU
TO THE MOON
AND BACK.

4 With your second paint color and a clean sponge brush, paint over the entire piece of wood, including the painter's tape and the stickers. Paint carefully over the stickers to make sure they don't move. A stamping motion works best to ensure that the stickers don't budge. Set aside to dry for about 30 minutes.

LOVE YOU
MOON
AND BACK.

5 Once the paint is dry, remove the painter's tape and stickers slowly to reveal the finished product!

6 If you've decided to hang your sign, you need to add a wire to the back of the sign for a hanger. Take your craft wire and bend it slightly, then use your glue gun to glue it to the back of the sign.

Make It Personal!

Check out Brandy signs online for quote ideas to put on your sign. My favorite way to find a quote is by searching "cute quotes" and looking at the images that show up in the search results. You can pick a quote that's long or short; just be sure that it will fit on the wooden board you are using. If you aren't sure whether a quote will fit, you can always check by laying out the quote with stickers before you stick them down.

WASHI TAPE DOOR

This is the perfect low-cost, noncommitment project to enhance your room. If you don't want to use paint to make your room colorful, washi tape is the next best thing. Washi tape can be used all around your room to add a little something here and there. Use it to make frames or fun geometric prints. Then, whenever you get tired of them, peel them off and start again!

materials ◉◉◉◉◉◉◉◉

- Washi tape rolls in assorted colors

1 To create a washi tape door design, first pick a point on the door to start. The door in the photos has raised surfaces with grooves in it, so I started by outlining those with washi tape, ripping the tape when I needed to switch direction.

2 Once you have outlined the raised surfaces, use 3 strips of washi tape to make a triangle in several of the enclosed sections that were created in the first step.

3 This project is open to your interpretation so let your imagination run wild and make something that fits your style.

Make It Personal!

Adding a few washi tape triangles or even a zigzag pattern would be a great addition to any space in your room! And remember, washi tape is easy to change up, so you won't be stuck with the same design for too long. If your door is flat, create the look of grooves by outlining two separate columns, each with a small square at the top and two tall rectangles at the bottom that cover the rest of the length of the door. It will look best if you start a few inches in from the outer edges of the door.

OMBRÉ PAINTED CANVAS

Ombré isn't just for hair anymore! Now you can showcase your inner artist with this fun Ombré Painted Canvas that is super easy to create. With a little mixing, you are sure to get the perfect ombré in no time. This goes perfectly with any room, because you can simply choose different paint colors to work with! This will look great over your desk or leaning on your nightstand.

materials

- 1 (14" × 19") canvas
- 4 bottles acrylic paint (3 shades of one color, plus white)
- 1 (½") paintbrush
- 1 pushpin (optional)

1 Start by using a bit of the darkest paint to mark how far out on each side of the canvas you want your ombré to go. I left about an inch of space at the outer edges.

Make It Personal!

The paint at the craft store will probably be lined up according to color, so pick shades on the shelf that are next to each other to guarantee an excellent ombré effect. Picking similar shades is what ombré is all about. As far as colors go, choose shades that match or complement your room.

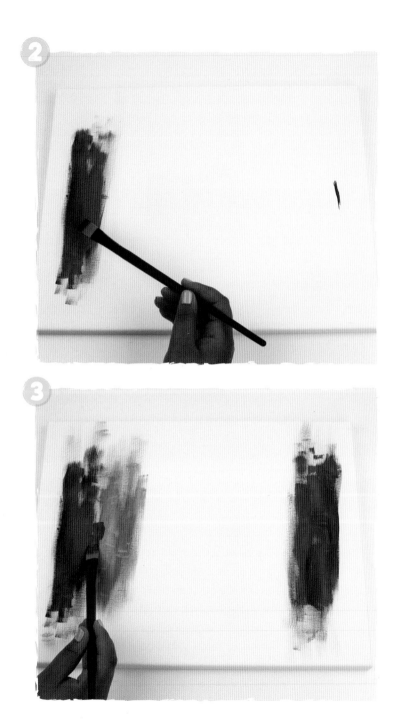

2 Starting at those markings, use long strokes of your paintbrush to paint stripes of the darkest color on the outer edges, working toward the middle of the canvas switching shades every 1½" to 2".

3 Each time you switch shades, lightly blend the line where the colors meet for a nice, even look. There's no need to wash your brush between each color; leaving a little bit of the previous paint color on the brush helps to make everything look blended.

4 When you get to the middle of the canvas, take the lightest shade mixed with a bit of white paint to transition between colors in the center.

5 Give the paint plenty of time to dry, about 40 minutes. Then, if desired, use a pushpin to hang up your masterpiece!

CHALKBOARD FRAME

There is something about a good, old-fashioned chalkboard that makes you want to write cute little reminders. And this Chalkboard Frame is so adorable that you'll love scribbling things on your board—and so will your friends! This insanely easy project is great if you're always forgetting to do things. So keep your memory fresh and have fun doodling on this cute little chalkboard!

materials

- 1 (12" × 17") frame
- 1 (17.7" × 51.1" roll) vinyl chalkboard surface with an adhesive backing
- Chalk
- Scissors

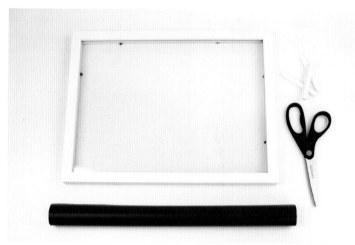

1 Start by opening up your frame, removing the glass, and setting the frame aside.

2 Roll out your vinyl chalkboard surface and place the glass on top. To ensure you have enough vinyl to cover the glass entirely, mark the edges of the glass on the vinyl with chalk, leaving an extra inch on each side for wrapping. The vinyl surface should measure about 13" × 18".

3 Using scissors, trim the vinyl.

Make It Personal!

To jazz up the edges of the frame your chalkboard is in why not add on a few gems or a few extra flowers you have on hand. You can do this by adding a drop of glue to any small decoration you want to add. Anything you decide to do will give your chalkboard the awesome personal touch that will make it stand out!

4 Slowly and carefully remove the vinyl from its backing and smooth it out over the glass so that there are no air bubbles. It is best to apply the vinyl chalkboard from the top or bottom edge of the glass, rather than plopping it down on top of the entire piece. Slowly smooth the vinyl surface down and outward with your finger as you lay it down. If you do happen to get an air bubble, just lift the vinyl up and carefully reapply to the spot that needs to be smoothed.

5 When the front is free of air bubbles, tuck the excess edges of the vinyl behind the glass so they are hidden from view. You should be left with a smooth chalkboard surface that you can pop back into the frame.

6 You can start using your chalkboard immediately, with no priming or dry time—like you'd need if you used chalkboard paint!

SEQUIN HEART

If you're the sparkly type, then this project is the one for you! Add a little—actually, a lot—of sparkle to your room with this adorable Sequin Heart! When light hits the shiny sequins, it creates a magical effect with sequin-colored reflections dancing around the room. It is so easy to do you'll wonder why you didn't do it before. You'll only need to grab a few supplies, and you'll be done in no time!

materials

- 1 (8" × 10") cardboard heart
- Roughly 60 (40-millimeter) large sequin disks
- Roughly 60 thumbtacks in the same color as the sequins
- Mounting tape (optional)

1 Starting at the base of the heart and working upward, push a thumbtack through the top of a sequin and into the cardboard heart, about three-quarters of the way through the cardboard surface. Make sure to not completely pin down the sequin, so that it has a bit of movement to it.

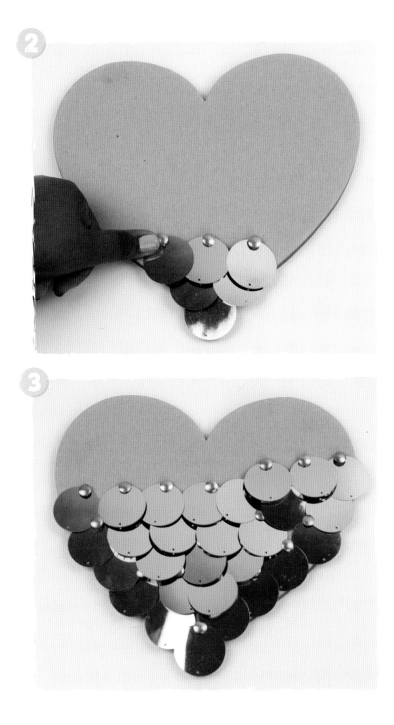

2 Add your sequins to the cardboard heart in rows as you work your way up, slightly overlapping the sequins to cover the thumbtacks in the previous row. Add an additional sequin to each row.

3 As you get up to the curved sections near the top of the heart, it is even more important to work in straight lines for a polished look. Keep working left to right in even rows to keep the pattern consistent.

4 Once you've finished adding the sequins, use the mounting tape to mount the Sequin Heart to your wall, if desired.

Make It Personal!

This project looks great when you use flat thumbtacks, and not pushpins. You can use the same color thumbtacks as sequins for a uniform look, or switch things up and make it colorful. Thumbtacks of all colors can be found at office supply stores or craft stores. If you can't find the perfect color, you can buy silver thumbtacks and go over them with a layer of spray paint before you get started.

FAUX FLOWER MONOGRAM

Bring on spring with this Faux Flower Monogram, which adds pretty blooms to your décor. Flowers liven up any space, and this project is no exception. You can buy a few bunches of your favorite faux flowers and mix in a couple of different paper flowers to make this project even more affordable. Hang it on the wall with a frilly ribbon, or, for ultimate flower power, use a fabric flower ribbon!

materials

- 1 wooden letter (any size)
- 50 faux flowers (without stems)
- Glue gun
- 6" floral lace trim or ribbon (any width)

1 On a flat work surface, lay out your letter and arrange your flowers where you want them to go. Start with the larger flowers first, placing them near the center of the letter, then work your way outward, filling in the spaces with medium-sized flowers. Be careful not to go too far over the edges of the letter; this will help maintain the shape of the letter. This is just to get an idea of how it will look, so don't glue them down just yet!

2 Once you are satisfied with the look you've created, remove the flowers and use your glue gun to attach them to the letter in your preferred pattern.

3 To hang this up, add a bit of glue to both ends of the ribbon, then stick those glued ends to the back of the letter. Allow the glue to dry for about 10 minutes, and then you'll be ready to hang it up!

Make It Personal!

Glue faux flowers to the first letter of your name—or even better, to your initials—to make a classy monogram.

HANGING DECORATIONS

CH2

Now that you've made some amazing flat wall art in Chapter 1, it's time for you to move your DIY game into the next dimension and make some amazing 3D hanging decorations! In this chapter, you'll learn how to make dazzling garlands that add a little party to your personal space, functional and fashionable hanging storage to keep your stuff off the floor, creative and fun art pieces, and lots more. So, if you want to add a fun, hip twist to your walls with some dangly décor, these are the projects for you! Let's get crafting!

CLOTHESPIN PICTURES

If you have tons of pictures lying around (or want some more!), this frameless look is a cute way to display them and fill up some space on your wall. And there's no need to use dull, boring, wood-colored clothespins here. This project teaches you how to jazz them up by adding rhinestones, gems, glitter, and sequins! Take DIY wall décor to the next level by adding lights along the string for an enchanting look! Once they are up, you can lie in bed and admire your wonderful walls while you nod off to sleep.

materials

- Digital images
- Photo paper (plain printer paper works, too)
- Scissors
- 1 roll 12-gauge wire
- Varied colors and shapes of loose or self-adhesive rhinestones/gems (approx. 1–5 per clothespin)
- Glue gun
- Clothespins (2 per photo)
- 2 pushpins

1 Open up some of your favorite photos on your computer (feel free to pull from your digital photos, Instagram, Tumblr pictures, or more!) and resize them so they are all 4" × 6". You can arrange multiple pictures on one page to save paper. Once your photos are all the same size, print them, and use the scissors to cut them out.

2 Measure out enough wire to accommodate all of your pictures, with 6" extra on each end to hang it up.

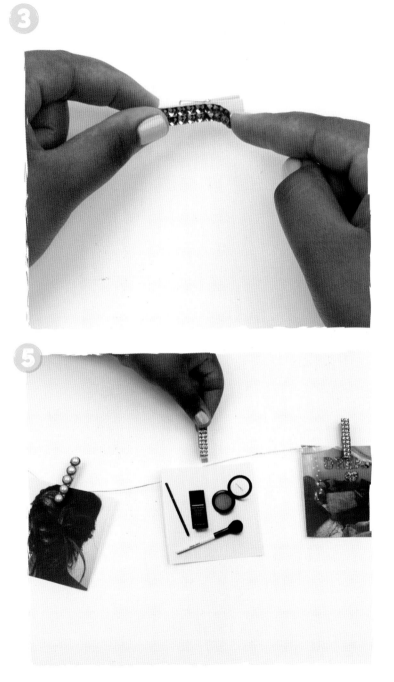

3 Next, use self-adhesive rhinestones or use your glue gun to attach gems to the face of the clothespins.

4 Wrap each end of the wire around a pushpin, and use the pushpins to hang it up on the wall.

5 Clip all of your pictures onto the wire with the clothespins, using 2 per picture, and enjoy!

MULTI-COLORED YARN HANGING

You don't have to know how to knit to make yarn look good. All it takes is a dose of creativity and some simple techniques to complete this project—you only need to learn one simple knot! This yarn hanging adds an awesome touch just about anywhere in your room. It'll go great hung in that reading nook, or just on your wall! You can mix up the colors of the yarn for a multicolored effect, or create one that's all the same color—either way, you're going to love the result. Whichever direction you decide to go in, you can't go wrong with this fun and fuzzy project!

materials

- 150 yards yarn (all one color, or mixed)
- Ruler
- Scissors
- Scotch tape (optional)

1 Measure and cut a 48" piece of yarn. This will be your anchor strand.

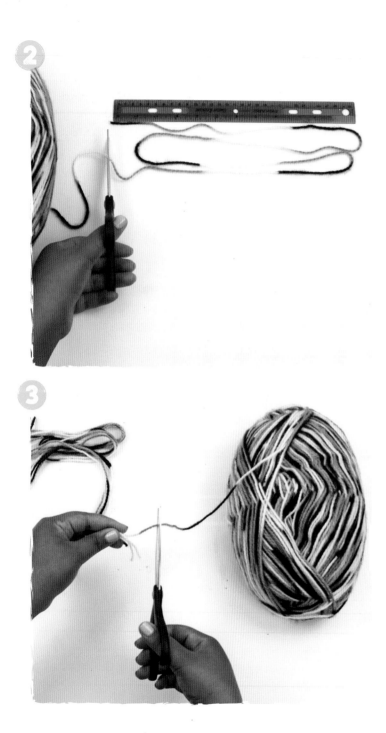

2 Next, measure and cut a second 48" strand of yarn. This will be your first hanging strand.

3 Using the hanging strand you cut in the previous step as a guide, cut 99 additional hanging strands for a total of 100. You don't need to measure each one individually if you use this method, which should save you a lot of time.

4 Once you have all of your hanging strands cut, fold one in half, meeting the two ends together so you are left with a loop at the top.

5 With your anchor strand laying straight and flat, slide the looped end of the hanging strand under the anchor strand so that the loop extends about 1" above the anchor strand. (See following photo.)

6 Guide the two loose ends of the hanging strand over the anchor strand and through the loop, then pull tight to complete the knot. Repeat this looping, laying, and knotting process until you have used up all of your hanging strands, or until you are happy with the width of yarn. I had an excess of 7" of anchor stand left on each side when I was done.

7 You can leave this as is, or you can trim the hanging strands into a triangle shape at the bottom. To do this, make sure all of the strands are lined up evenly by combing through them with your fingers. Then, starting at one side, take your scissors and cut the hanging strands on a diagonal until you get to the center of the hanging strands. Repeat this on the other side until both sides meet at a point in the middle.

8 If desired, tape the ends of the anchor strand to the wall. I chose to hang mine loosely in a U shape, but you can pull the anchor strand taut if you wish.

DREAM CATCHER

It's time to squash that recurring nightmare of showing up to school in your underwear with this trendy take on a dream catcher. Dream catchers are all over Tumblr and Pinterest, but can be so expensive to buy; this is an easy way to make your own that doesn't require a lot of work. Just add some beads here and some feathers there, and you'll be avoiding bad dreams while making your room as hip as ever!

materials

- 1 plastic embroidery hoop (any size)
- A lace doily large enough to stretch over the embroidery hoop
- Scissors
- Assorted colors/styles of ribbon (approx. 12"–18" per color/style)
- Glue gun
- 6–12 assorted beads in colors/styles that complement your ribbon
- 2 or 3 feathers
- Pushpin (optional)

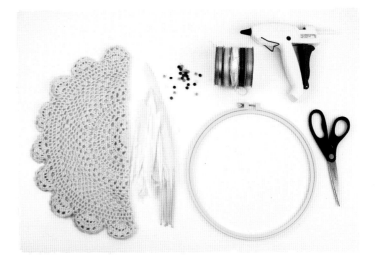

1 Open up your embroidery hoop by loosening the screw and removing the outer ring.

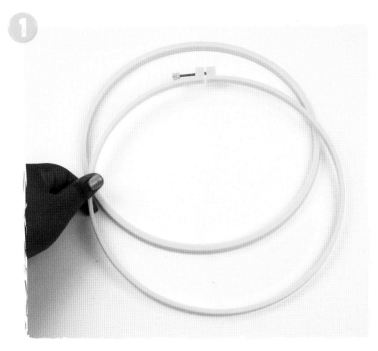

2 Center the doily over the inner ring, then replace the outer hoop and tighten the screw so the lace stays locked in place.

3 Flip the hoop over and cut off the extra lace that sticks out from the edges. Leave a small fringe to ensure that the lace does not fall out of the hoop.

4 Begin cutting your ribbons to several different lengths to add to the Dream Catcher. The number of ribbons and the lengths are totally up to you, but it looks best when there is a mixture of long (approx. 9") and short (approx. 6") strands in each color.

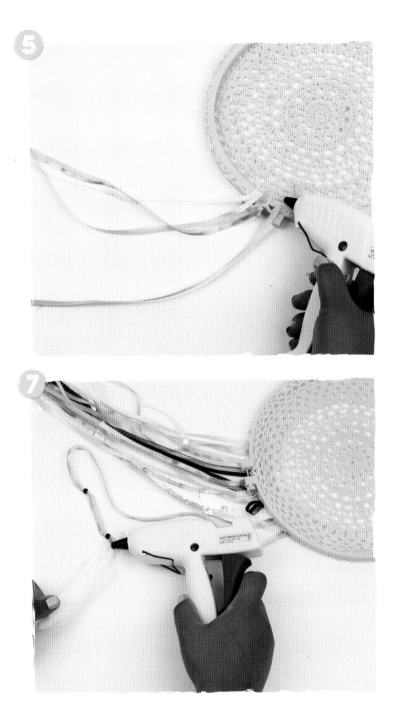

5 Leaving the hoop face down, glue your ribbons to the section of the embroidery hoop that has the screw tightener for more space to glue. Make sure to alternate between colors and lengths of ribbon for the best look!

6 Once all of your ribbons are glued in place, begin adding beads by stringing them onto the ribbon. My beads were small enough to stay on the ribbon without adding knots, but if yours have larger holes, make a knot after each bead. Again, the number of beads you add to the ribbons is entirely up to you, but I like to add 2 or 3 beads to 3 or 4 ribbons to give the Dream Catcher a unique look.

7 Now, use your glue gun to glue feathers to the ends of some of the ribbons. Once you add a feather to a ribbon you will not be able to add more beads, so make sure you finish with your beads before beginning this step. Allow your glue to dry for about 1 to 2 minutes, then your new Dream Catcher is complete! If desired, hang it above your bed on a pushpin and, *poof*, your nightmares will be gone!

ANTLER JEWELRY HOLDER

What if there was a way for you to never deal with tangled necklaces ever again? Sounds awesome, right? Well, this Antler Jewelry Holder is the answer to your prayers! Storing your necklaces this way makes for easy access and is the ultimate time saver. Antlers are huge right now, and painting these ones gold gives them just the right look! This isn't just for necklaces—it's also the perfect resting place for scarves and purses!

materials

- Newspaper or cardboard to protect floor (optional)
- 1 set resin antlers
- 1 can spray paint (any color)
- Masking tape
- 2 acrylic paint colors
- 1 small craft paintbrush (approx. ½")
- Mounting tape (optional)
- 2 thumbtacks (optional)

1 In a well-ventilated area, lay down paper or cardboard to protect the ground if desired, and coat your antlers evenly with spray paint. Allow to dry for about 2 hours. This may require a second coat; just be sure to wait until they are completely dry before going on!

2 Once the spray paint has dried, use the masking tape to tape off small sections at the end of the antlers, leaving just the tips exposed.

3 Use a brush to apply the acrylic paint to the exposed tips and set the antler aside to dry for about 30 minutes. Paint some of the tips with one color of paint, and some with the other. You may need to use two coats to make the paint look opaque. Again, just be patient in waiting for your paint to dry before adding another layer!

4 After everything is completely dry, which will probably take up to a full day, remove the tape and start hanging pretty scarves and precious jewels on your Antler Jewelry Holder! My antlers came with hooks for thumbtacks; if yours don't have those hooks, feel free to use mounting tape.

Make It Personal!

Can't use spray paint? Don't worry about it! Regular paint might take a bit longer to apply all over the antlers, but you can get the same effect!

MOTIVATIONAL QUOTE PENNANT

We could all use a little motivation . . . especially the Monday morning "I need to get up" kind of motivation. Hang this Motivational Quote Pennant right above your nightstand or on your closet door so you'll see it first thing in the morning. You'll be surprised how it can change your mood, or give you a little boost to get going when you need it most! Choose a quote that makes you smile when you see it. Search online for some awesome ideas for quotes, or use something like "It's O.K." or "Good morning, sunshine" to pep you up just enough to take on the day!

materials

- 1 (8" × 8") piece of felt
- Letter stickers (see Step 1 for the size)
- Scissors
- Acrylic paint in a color that can be seen on the felt
- 1 (1") sponge brush
- 10" twine
- Thumbtack or pushpin (optional)

1 Decide which quote you want to use, then arrange your letter stickers on the felt to make sure it will fit with at least 1" to 2" to spare. There is nothing worse than realizing that you don't have enough room! This is just to get an idea of where to place them; don't peel the backing off yet. If you are using a short quote, feel free to choose larger letter stickers; if you pick a long quote, choose smaller letter stickers.

2 To create a pennant shape, take your felt and fold it in half. Make a 45-degree cut diagonally across from the bottom of

the folded edge up toward about the middle of the open edge. When you unfold the felt, you will have created the triangle shape at the bottom of the pennant.

3 Now you can go ahead and stick your stickers on the felt, making sure they are fully secure before you start to paint.

4 Begin by using a sponge brush to pat on the paint, over and around the letters. You don't have to worry too much about making the paint even; this is more of a sponge painting look, so you want it to be kind of messy! Once you've finished painting, allow the paint to completely dry (for about 30 minutes), then peel off the letter stickers.

5 Next, use your scissors to make a small X-shaped cut on each of the top two corners by pinching the felt to fold it and then making small snips.

6 String your twine through the holes. Pull one end of the twine halfway through one hole, then repeat with the second end of twine and the other hole so that there is an even length of twine on the front and back. Tie the two ends of twine together to make a loop on the front and another on the back. Hang both loops over a thumbtack or pushpin, and your Motivational Quote Pennant is ready to inspire!

GLITTER-DIPPED FEATHER GARLAND

If you want to incorporate feathers into your bedroom décor, then this super-cute feather garland is for you. But this project doesn't stop there! It goes one step beyond and gives your garland a glitter-dipped look in just minutes. Choose any color of glitter that your heart desires, and you'll be completely obsessed with how this looks. Match the garland to your room by choosing a colored glitter that goes well with your room theme. It would look awesome with blue, or even purple!

materials

- 7–10 white feathers (any size)
- 2 (1") sponge brushes
- Mod Podge
- 1 paper plate (any size)
- 1 (3-ounce) jar of glitter
- Glue gun
- 3' twine
- Scotch tape (optional)

1 For the feathers: Using the sponge brush over a paper plate, apply Mod Podge onto the bottom half of the feather in downward strokes, making sure to wipe off any excess with the sponge brush. You don't need a lot for the glitter to stick. Do this to both the front and back of the feather.

2 Next, pour on your choice of glitter over the layer of Mod Podge and tap off the excess over the paper plate. Repeat this process on the other side of the feather, put aside to dry, then repeat for all the feathers you want to use for your garland. I did about 10 feathers this way.

3 Once your feathers have dried (an hour or so), use your sponge brush to apply a final coat of Mod Podge over the top of the glitter to seal it in, then let that sit 15 to 20 minutes or until the Mod Podge is clear or dry to the touch.

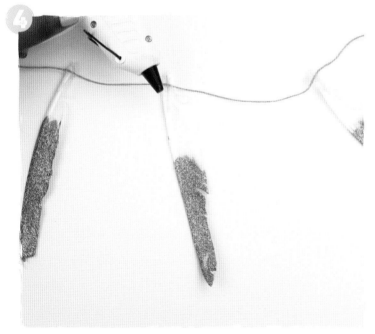

4 For the garland: Add a bit of hot glue to the stem of the feather, then press the feather down onto the twine. Repeat with all of your remaining feathers, being sure to space them evenly. Leave a few extra inches of twine on each end so you can attach the garland to the wall with Scotch tape, if desired.

TASSEL GARLAND

Tassel Garlands that bring the party work well all year round, and are probably my favorite room accessory. Make one with colored tissue paper, or add a few silver and gold metallic tassels if you're feeling fancy! It's so much fun to change up the color scheme to really make a statement. This project takes a little time, but the end result is so worth it! After all, who says your room can't be a party 24/7?

materials

- Tissue paper (3 or 4 sheets)
- Rotary cutter
- Scissors
- Scotch tape
- 24" twine

1 Take one sheet of tissue paper and fold it in half lengthwise away from you. Next, turn the tissue paper 90 degrees and fold away from you widthwise so that the seam is at the top. You will want to make sure to carefully line up the edges so everything stays in place.

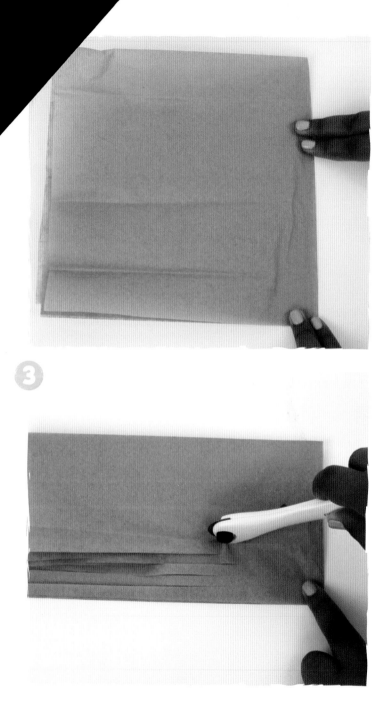

2 Before making this last fold, turn the folded tissue paper so the seam is facing toward you and the open end facing away. Now, fold the paper in half from left to right like a book.

3 Once your folds are in place, use your rotary cutter to create the tassels by cutting vertically up toward the seam, leaving a little less than 2" uncut at the top.

4 After you have made the cuts, unfold the paper once, then cut up the middle crease with the scissors. This will leave you with four separate pieces that will each become tassels.

5 Take one of your sections and start twisting the uncut middle portion of the tissue paper, being careful not to rip it. Make sure that the tassel end does not get tangled up while you twist.

6 Make a loop with the twisted section, then add a piece of tape to secure it.

7 Now, string your twine through the loop in each tassel, hang it up with Scotch tape, and say hello to your Tassel Garland!

CH3

DIY DESKTOP DÉCOR

Let's be honest, you probably spend a lot of time at your desk doing things that might not be that fun . . . like papers, or studying, or other types of homework. But since you have to put in the time, you may as well be resourceful and turn your dull desk into an amazing DIY space with the projects found in this chapter! Here you'll learn how to amp up existing organizational items like trays and mugs, and really make them cute as well as functional. You wouldn't want to leave your bureau behind in all of this DIY fun, so you'll also find projects to display there to bring it from boring to glam, to match your new DIY desk décor. By adding some pompoms here and some rhinestones there, these projects are guaranteed to make even the most boring items into sparkly and fun decorations! Let's get started!

MAGNETIC MAKEUP ORGANIZER

Stumped on where to store your favorite lip gloss or blush? Then declutter your collection with this Magnetic Makeup Organizer. Now you can display your favorite makeup in a single organized place, while hardly taking up any space at all. Magnetize your most frequently used items so that they're always within reach to guarantee that you'll never lose your favorites. Once you start using this, you won't want to stop! You'll want to add magnets to any and everything to fill your board!

materials

- Glue gun
- Coin magnets, 1 per item you want to hang
- Makeup/miscellaneous items
- Magnetic board
- 2 thumbtacks or pushpins (optional)

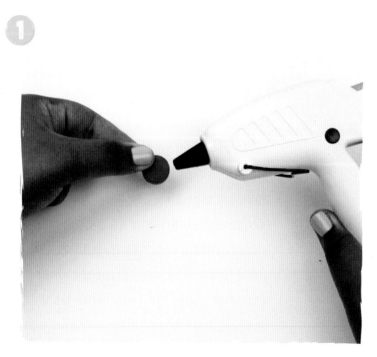

1 Start by adding a drop of glue to the back of one of the coin magnets.

Make It Personal!

You can easily find magnetic boards at the craft store, but IKEA has great options in their office section as well.

2 Before the glue dries, press your makeup item against the glue and hold it tight for 10 to 15 seconds. Make sure you glue the magnet to a part of the makeup that will not get in your way while using it. For lipstick, add the magnet to the cap, and for a makeup brush, place it near the bristles where you don't hold it.

3 If desired, use a thumbtack or pushpin to hang your magnetic board, where you do your makeup for easy access. Stick the makeup on the board, and you are good to go!

GILDED GEOMETRIC PRINT POT

Nothing gets you motivated better than a cute workspace. Dress yours up and get organized with this shiny gold print pot. The geometric prints used in the project are totally in style and make for a useful desk accessory that is 100 percent your own creation! This metallic gold geometric printed pot is easy to customize, and works well to store pens and pencils or whatever else you have on your desk. There are all kinds of possibilities for fun designs just waiting to be discovered, so get creative with your painter's tape and make new designs simply by switching up the placement. You can make your gold print pot both unique and awesome!

materials

- Garden pot (any size)
- 1 roll 3/4"–1" painter's tape
- Stencil (optional)
- Gold liquid gilding
- 1 (1") sponge brush

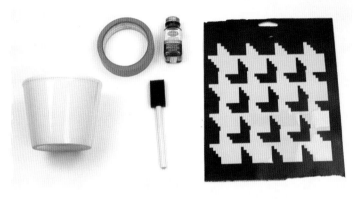

1 First, place the pot on its side and apply painter's tape in two parallel, diagonal lines to the side of the pot, spaced about 1/2" apart. Make sure you smooth the tape down completely against the pot to prevent any paint from getting under it.

2 Next, starting from the middle of the second tape strip, add a third piece of tape perpendicular to the first, going diagonally toward the bottom of the pot. If you have a stencil you want to use, tape that on the pot in the place you want instead of applying painter's tape. (See following image.)

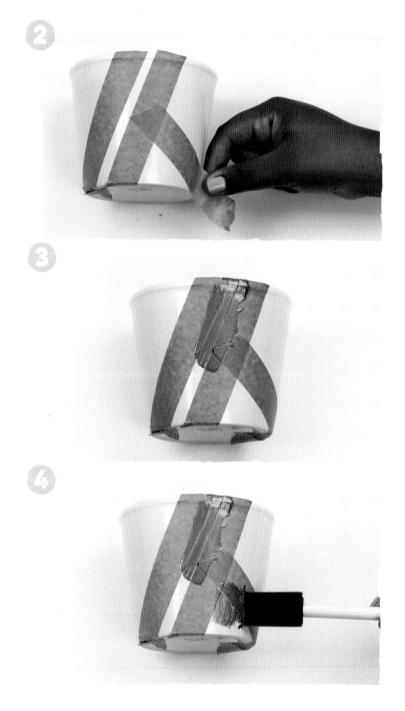

3 Begin painting the gold between the parallel pieces of painter's tape, making sure not to get any paint outside of the border they create.

4 Paint the lower section created by the third piece of painter's tape, then set the pot aside to dry for about 20 minutes, or for the specified drying time on the jar of paint.

5 Once the paint is completely dry, slowly and carefully remove the painter's tape from the pot to reveal your gold geometric pattern.

6 Now you are ready to get organized, so add your pens, pencils, or anything that needs to be stored!

Make It Personal!

This project shows you one way to create a pattern on your pot, but you can unlock a ton of others just by adding more tape strips or laying tape on the pot in different ways. Stripes, triangles, squares, you name it! The possibilities are endless!

ROPE PENCIL HOLDER

Give a simple tin can new life by turning it into a cute and practical desk organizer in this Rope Pencil Holder project. If you're looking for another way to store all of your pens and pencils, this project is perfect! Plus it's a great way to recycle stuff you probably already have on hand. I love the nautical look of this pencil holder, but if that's not your thing, add lace or cover the outside with funky scrapbook paper instead!

materials

- 2½" × 4" tin can
- 2 yards cording (any size)
- Glue gun
- Scissors

1 Starting from the bottom of the can, use a large dollop of glue to attach one end of the cording to the can. This will be the back of the can; there will be a small empty space at the bottom, since the rope goes in a spiral around the can, but don't worry about that.

2 Add glue to the can in long lines, moving in an upward spiral. Press and hold the cording down as you go, so that it sticks. Make sure that each level of cord is flush with the previous one, and that there are no gaps between rows.

3 Once the wrapped cord reaches the top of the can, secure the cord with a final dot of glue. If there is any extra cord at the end, trim it off and make sure that it is properly secured to the back of the can on the same side that you secured the end of the cording at the beginning.

Make It Personal!

You can use any size can that you'd like for this project! If you have something bigger or smaller than what's called for in the instructions, just measure out your cording by wrapping it around the container you are working with to ensure you have enough to cover the entire thing. Even if you have more cording than you think you need, don't cut it until the end of the project to avoid running out.

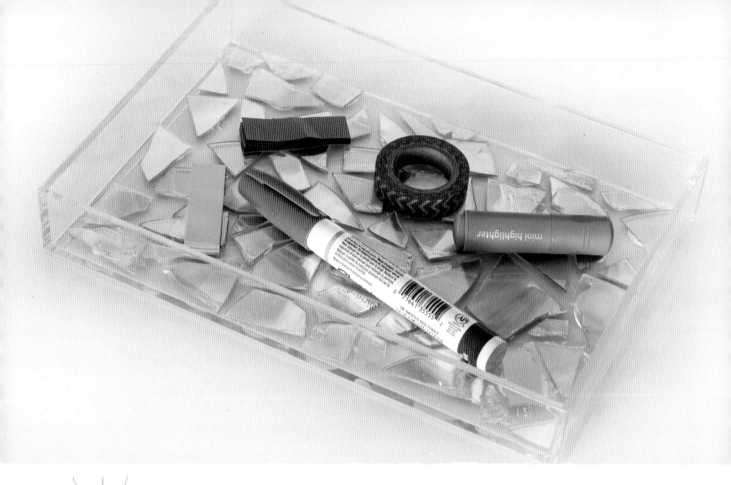

SHINY MOSAIC TRAY

Do you love repurposing items that you already have lying around the house and turning them into something new? Here you'll transform old CDs into a shiny and stylish tray that you can use to store all kinds of things, from jewelry, hair clips, and ties to pens, pencils, and Post-its to anything you can't find a place for. If you're not sure where to find old CDs, ask your parents or hit up your local thrift store. Just make sure you don't pick an artist that you actually like, or you might regret destroying it!

materials

- 5 CDs
- Scissors
- 1 (10" × 6") acrylic tray
- Glue gun

1 Use your scissors to cut the CDs into small squares, triangles, rectangles, and other shapes. Try not to make them too elaborate since they will fit together later; think of the CD shards as puzzle pieces.

2 Once cut, separate your CD shards into groups of small and large pieces. The small pieces will be useful on the outer edges, or when filling in open spaces that may occur later. Large pieces are better suited for the inner portion of the tray.

3 Take your tray and, with the silver side up, glue the CD pieces into the bottom, starting at the outer sides. Try your best to fit them together, leaving small spaces between each one so that you can still see the bottom of the tray. When laying the pieces down, use triangular pieces to fit into small spaces, and use square pieces to cover large areas. Not all of the shards will fit together perfectly, and that's okay. The main thing you want to worry about is getting the majority of the tray covered.

4 Once you have laid out your pieces, use the small shards to fill in any gaps. Wait about 20 minutes for the glue to dry, then use your new shiny tray to hold your paperclips, erasers, a USB drive, and more!

STUDDED TRAY

If you can never seem to find anything on your desk, then this Studded Tray is a must-have for keeping mess in check. Adding studs to a plain paper tray gives it just the right amount of edge and makes it look totally awesome when it's on display. And it works as the perfect catchall for all of your junk—er, important papers. This project is a cinch to complete, and because the tray is adorable, you'll end up organized in no time.

materials

- 1 (10" × 6") acrylic tray
- 24 flat-back studs
- Glue gun

1 Start out by laying out your studs, about 1" apart, along the outside edges of the tray.

2 Leaving your studs in the spacing, pick up one at a time and apply a small drop of glue to the back of the stud, and carefully replace it. Press down on the stud firmly for about 5 seconds to give the glue time to adhere.

3 Repeat until all sides of the tray are covered in studs, then enjoy!

RHINESTONE LETTER BOOKENDS

If you love to read, but find that your books are always falling over and cluttering up your room, just make some custom bookends to keep your books up and add a bit of flair to your book display. You can cover your bookends with anything you want, from scrapbook paper to acrylic paint! This project uses rhinestones, but if they aren't your thing, studs, or even scrapbook paper and a bit of Mod Podge, would look great. These bookends will add that extra little touch to your books and make you want to sit down and read—especially if your mini-library comes with its own reading nook!

materials

- 2 (8") wooden letters/symbols
- 4 (4"× 4") adhesive rhinestone sheets
- Utility knife (such as an X-Acto)

1 Start by laying your rhinestone sheet against the wooden letter. Leave on the backing so you can decide where you want to place it first.

2 Peel the backing off of the rhinestone sheet and stick it down to the wooden letter.

3 Use the utility knife to cut off any parts of the rhinestone sheet that are sticking over the edges or covering the inside spaces of the letter.

4 Reuse the excess pieces that you cut off as needed to fill in any empty spaces on the letter. Feel free to use more than one full sheet, if necessary. Repeat the same process with your second wooden shape or symbol. Place the bookends on your shelf to keep those books in line!

INITIAL MUG PEN HOLDER

The best way to stay organized on your desk is to have plenty of storage space. If your pens and pencils are flying free—under your desk, most likely—this custom initial mug turned pen holder is perfect for you. Since it has your initials, you can even bring it to school if you have some desk space of your own to show off your craftiness! Wherever it ends up, you (or whoever gets to see it) will love the simple yet stylish look of this project!

materials

- Letter stencil
- Plain white mug
- Scotch tape
- Sharpie oil-based paint marker

1 Start by attaching the outer edges of your letter stencil onto your mug using the Scotch tape. This will make it easier to paint without worrying about the stencil moving around. It may take a little work to get the stencil to lie flat on the curved surface of the cup, so take your time making sure everything looks good before moving on.

2 Next, begin coloring inside the stencil with your paint marker. If you need to, hold down the inside edges of the stencil with the hand you are not painting with to get a cleaner line.

3 After you have filled in the stencil, carefully remove it from the cup.

4 Now, use the Sharpie marker to touch up any parts of the paint that do not look completely solid. Once you're happy with the coverage, set the mug aside to dry for about 10 minutes, then drop in your pens and pencils and enjoy!

Make It Personal!

Make this project unique by freehanding your own creative design on the cup, or going for a flower or butterfly stencil to personalize it. Remember, these cups are great for storing pens but aren't safe to drink out of due to the oil-based paints that are used!

CAKE TRAY
JEWELRY STAND

This jewelry stand, designed to look like a cake tray, is great for storing all of your wayward rings, bracelets, and earrings. You can make it girly and dainty with some decorative white plates, or let your jewelry really shine with a metal or mirrored plate. Thrift stores are the perfect place to find cool plates and stands, so check them out and choose pieces that you love! This stand is customizable, so no matter what you like, this piece will be perfect!

materials

- 1 plate (any size)
- 1 wide, shallow-topped candlestick holder
- Glue gun

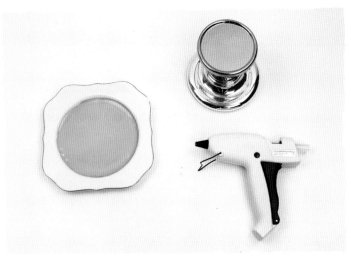

1 To start, set the plate on top of the candleholder to make sure it sits flat on top. Note: It's a good idea to pick out your candleholder at the same time as you choose your plate to ensure an even fit before you purchase your materials.

2 Once you get the right fit, line the rim and the entire top of the candleholder with glue.

3 Before the glue has a chance to dry, press the plate on top of the glue. Hold it down and wait 15 to 20 minutes for the glue to set. Once everything is dry your new jewelry stand is complete! Use it to display all of your favorite necklaces and bracelets!

Make It Personal!

If desired, add another tier with another candleholder and another plate to create a taller stand, which can house more jewelry. If you do decide to go taller, use a shorter candleholder and a plate that is smaller than the first one, so that you will be able to easily access all of the jewelry on both tiers.

POMPOM MOUSEPAD

You probably spend a lot of time at your desk, which means that you should get the most out of your decorating space! The mousepad is often overlooked as an item that can and should be decorated, but this project puts this desktop staple front and center. The pompoms used here give your mousepad the style it needs to compete with any of the other cool decorations on your desk. So get out those pompoms and take some time to DIY!

materials

- Mousepad
- Glue gun
- 30" string of pompoms
- Scissors

1 Start by applying a line of glue along the side edges of the mousepad. Be sure to not add too much glue, or you will have overflow when you go to add the pom-pom string.

2 Working on one side at a time, wrap your string of pompoms around the mousepad, carefully pressing it against the glue on the side edges as you go.

3 Once you have applied the pompom string all the way around, cut off the excess. Wait for the glue to dry for 10 minutes, and you're good to get back to work!

CH4

BEDSIDE BAUBLES

What is the first thing you should see when you wake up in the morning? Beautiful, fun, colorful items on your nightstand, that's what! So start your day off right by looking at the projects created from this chapter! They are dedicated to making your nightstand the best it can be by taking things you might already have there—like books or candles—and giving them a whole new life. Some simple crafting techniques are all you need to get these projects rolling, and soon you'll find yourself pumped up to start the day with a smile!

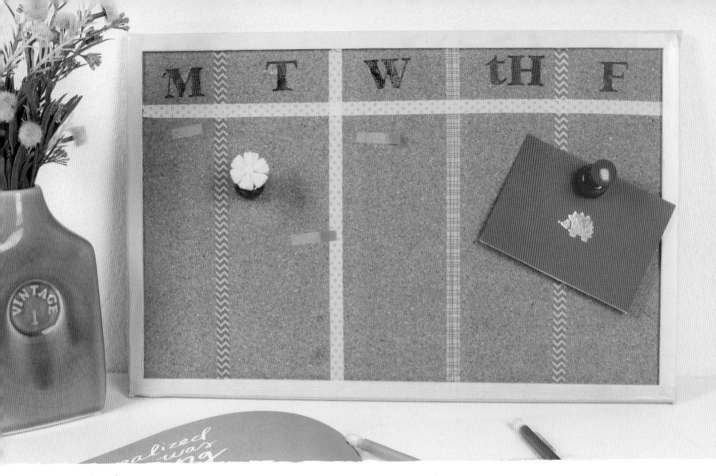

CORKBOARD CALENDAR

Using a calendar to keep track of important—and fun—dates and reminders is a great way to stay organized. Combining your calendar with a corkboard adds another level of usefulness and customizability that takes this DIY calendar to the next level. Here you'll use colorful washi tape as well as fun pushpins and tacks to amp up the level of cuteness on this calendar. You won't be able to resist making fun notes to your future self and keeping track of when your school assignments are due once this Corkboard Calendar is hanging on your wall!

materials

- 1 (11" × 17") cork bulletin board
- 5 washi tape rolls in assorted colors
- Ruler
- Letter stickers (roughly 2")

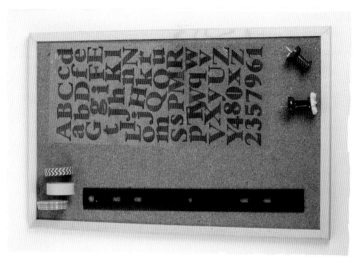

1 Take one roll of washi tape and use the tape to cover the wood or plastic frame surrounding your corkboard.

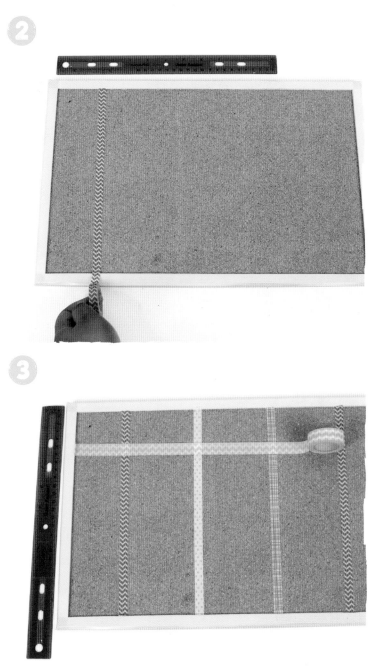

2 Next, lay your corkboard out horizontally, and use your ruler to measure out five equal columns of about 2½" each. Then, using other colors of washi tape, stick the tape onto the cork part of the corkboard at each 2½" interval, so that it forms a vertical column. Repeat to form a total of 5 columns.

3 Now, measure about 2" down from the top of the corkboard and run another color of washi tape vertically across the board on that line.

4 Use your letter stickers to label the boxes you've created at the top of the corkboard with the days of the week. I labeled mine with "M," "T," "W," "Th," and "F."

5 When all the stickers have been placed, put your Corkboard Calendar on your desk and dress it up with fun pushpins and colorful Post-it notes. Enjoy!

PERSONALIZED STICKER CANDLES

If you're addicted to candles in jars, this project is the perfect way to bring life back to old ones by making them part of your room décor. Get creative with prints and patterns—you can even print your monogram on one! Don't have candles lying around? Don't worry, empty jars or cans work the same way! Just make sure to change the size of your picture or pattern to fit the size of your container. These Personalized Sticker Candles are a fun and easy way to personalize your bedroom, and the best part? They're super easy to change up for different seasons, holidays, or whenever you're in the mood!

materials

- Candle in a jar
- Rubbing alcohol (optional)
- Cotton pad (optional)
- Printable sticker paper with printed pictures or patterns of your choice
- Scissors

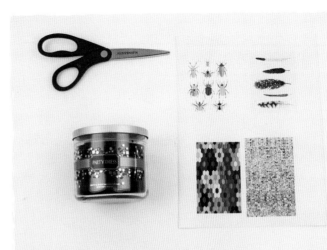

1 Start by removing the existing label from your candle jar. The label should be fairly easy to remove; if not, try using a bit of rubbing alcohol on a cotton ball to remove the sticky residue.

2 Next, cut the image or images that you had printed on your sticker paper to fit nicely on the front of your jar.

3 Remove the sticker backing and place the sticker onto the jar. Make sure to smooth all of the edges down firmly so your design lasts a long time!

PAINTED BOOKS

Cool fashion books are all the rage, and now you can create your own at a super-low price. Painting books is by far the best way to give them an entirely new look. You can personalize them even further by using stickers or by using a Sharpie to write on the spine of the book to amp up your creation. Display them on your nightstand on their own or with your other books to create a stylish display that looks like you spent a ton of money. Hey, maybe even pair them with the Rhinestone Letter Bookends from Chapter 3!

materials

- Books
- 2 paper towels
- 1 (2-ounce) bottle acrylic paint
- 1 (½") synthetic-bristle paintbrush
- Letter stickers or Sharpie (optional)

1 Start by removing the book jacket or anything on the outside of the book.

2 Open the book to the center pages, then lay it flat on the table with the cover and spine facing up. Place 1 paper towel between the front cover and the book pages, and 1 paper towel between the back cover and the book pages, to protect the pages and your workspace from paint.

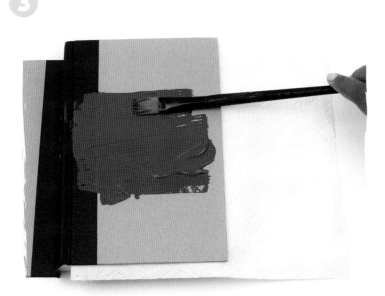

3 Load your brush up with paint and begin coating the book with long, even strokes. Allow it to dry for about 20 minutes. Once the paint is dry, you can apply a second coat if needed.

4 Personalize the spine of the book with stickers or write on it with a Sharpie. Have fun with it!

PAINTED FLOWER VASE

Who says it can't be spring all year round? No green thumb necessary! This Painted Flower Vase is so easy to make, and the painted inside will give your nightstand a unique look that you won't find anywhere else. If you don't need any more flowers in your room, use this vase to store pencils, pens, rulers, or anything that is long enough to stick out!

materials

- Clear vase
- 1 (2-ounce) bottle acrylic paint
- 1 (½") synthetic-bristle paintbrush (optional)
- Assorted faux flowers

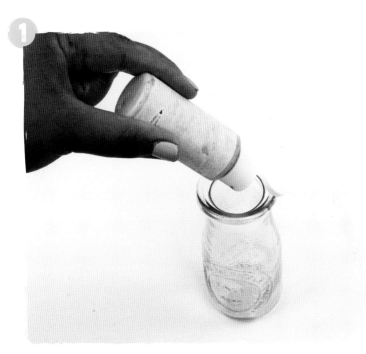

1 Start this off by pouring a good amount of paint into the vase, letting it pool on the bottom.

2 Then turn your vase sideways, rotating it so that the paint drips around the inside surface, coating it. Be patient, as the paint may drip slowly. As the paint runs down the sides, tilt the vase a bit further so that the paint runs as close to the rim as you want it to get. Add more paint if you need to; you may even end up using an entire bottle for one vase.

3 This vase basically paints itself, but you can fill in any gaps with a paintbrush to make sure the entire inside of the vase is covered. Let any excess paint drip out of the vase by turning it upside down. Set the vase right side up again and leave it until dry, which may take up to 24 hours, depending on how thick the paint is.

4 Once dry, add your favorite faux flowers and enjoy!

FIGURINE MASON JAR TOPPER

If you're looking for some fun and cute storage that can work anywhere around your room, look no further than these Mason jars with adorable painted figurines on top. Do you like cuddly fawns or lovable elephants? You're in luck! Pick your favorite animal to top your Mason jar to make it your own!

materials

- Mason jar
- Gold gilding paint
- 1 (1") sponge brush
- Miniature animal figurine
- Glue gun

1 Start by taking the lid off the Mason jar. If your lid has multiple pieces, separate them into two sections.

2 Paint both sections of the lid with the gilding paint and set aside to dry for about 10 minutes. Once the lid is dry, you can put both pieces back together and screw the lid back on the jar.

3 Next, paint the miniature animal figurine with the gilding paint, and set aside to dry for about 10 minutes as well.

4 Once the animal figurine is dry, use your glue gun to apply glue to the feet (or bottom) of the figurine, then place it on the middle of the Mason jar lid, pressing down for a few seconds. Set it aside to dry for about 30 minutes.

5 Once the glue is dry, this storage solution is ready for use. Fill your jar with lip balm, cell phone charger, glasses, or anything that you need on your nightstand.

MANNEQUIN HAND RING HOLDER

Stacking rings is totally on trend, and now displaying them can be, too. This Mannequin Hand Ring Holder is easy to make, and it definitely has an ultrahip vibe going on. You could leave the mannequin hand plain, or you could paint on a few palm-reading-style marks that make it look like something from a high-end store! You can even paint it a bright neon color to create a fun display piece that is both eye-catching and cool.

materials

- Mannequin hand
- Spray paint or acrylic paint
- 1 (1") sponge brush
- Black acrylic paint
- 1 (2-millimeter) small synthetic-bristle paintbrush

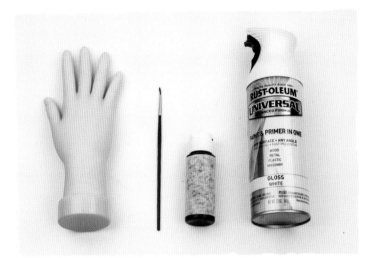

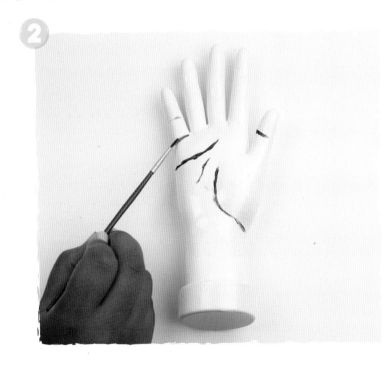

1 *If using spray paint:* Lay down newspaper or cardboard in a well-ventilated area and apply an even coat of spray paint to your mannequin hand. *If using acrylic paint:* Apply a few coats of acrylic paint to your mannequin hand to make sure to get even coverage, allowing each coat to dry for 20 minutes before applying the next coat. Set aside to dry for 1 hour.

2 Once your mannequin hand is dry, use your small paintbrush to add palm-reading markings to the hand in black paint. To do this, first make long black lines across the palm area that do not connect all the way to

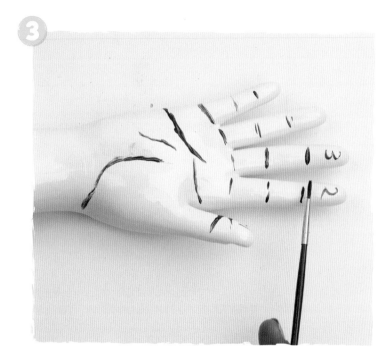

the other side. It's helpful if you look at your own hand to get an idea of where to draw the darkest lines. Pay attention to where your fingertips bend; that is where you will want to paint black lines on the fingers.

3 On the tip of each finger, you can paint the numbers 1 through 5, starting with the thumb. I also added little dots in random places to make it look cooler. Just feel it out, and add random squiggly lines and dashes wherever you feel like it. You can do an online search for "henna design" if you want to use a different kind of pattern.

4 Now, wait about 30 minutes for the paint to dry, and start stacking your rings!

Make It Personal!

Finding a mannequin hand at an online store like Amazon or eBay is your best bet. You can also search for them in the nail art section of a beauty supply store.

SUNBURST MIRROR

Sunburst mirrors can add light to any space! They're really trendy right now, which means they are also on the expensive side. But fear not, this project teaches you how to glam up an inexpensive round mirror using only pipe cleaners! This simple mirror modification turns a dull, round mirror into a happy, light, and fun piece of décor that you can hang above your nightstand! Who knew pipe cleaners could make something so cute?

materials

- 100 gold pipe cleaners
- 1 (9") frameless circular mirror
- Glue gun
- Mounting tape (optional)

1 Start by folding your pipe cleaners in half. You can do this in bunches to make the process faster.

2 After all of your pipe cleaners are folded, use your glue gun to glue the two loose ends to the back of the mirror, leaving two-thirds of the bent pipe cleaner visible from the front. Continue gluing pipe cleaners this way until you make it all the way around.

3 Gently arrange the pipe cleaners so that they are sticking straight out like a sun's rays around the mirror.

4 If desired, use mounting tape to hang the mirror at eye level so you can see yourself in the sunshine!

CH5

FANCY
FABRICS

Your walls look fantastic, your desk and bureau are organized, and your nightstand never looked better. Now it's time to make your bedding and curtains as totally amazing as the rest of your room!

In this chapter, you'll learn how to make some easy, affordable, and absolutely enticing DIYs for your bed and some flashy ideas for super-fun curtains that just scream ah-mazing! After all, who wouldn't want a Gold Pillowcase with a shimmering Sequin Curtain to go along with it? And why wouldn't you want to complement your décor with a Pompom Pillow and coordinating curtain, or get groovy with one that's dip-dyed? If you're crazy about bedding and curtains, you're sure to find something to love here!

POMPOM PILLOW

A bed is not complete without a million and one pillows, right? This project will teach you how to make your bed pop by adding pompoms to a plain pillow. Colored pompoms make for a great way to upcycle what you already have into something fresh and new, without having to go out and buy new pillows every time you get bored. And—even better—this project takes almost no time at all! What could be better than that?

materials

- 1 (16" × 16") pillow/pillow form
- 100–200 (½") loose small pompoms
- Glue gun

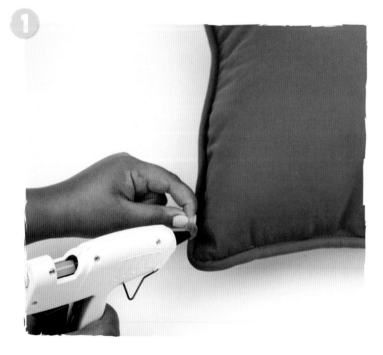

1 Use your glue gun to add a bit of glue to a pompom, then press it down onto a corner of the pillow.

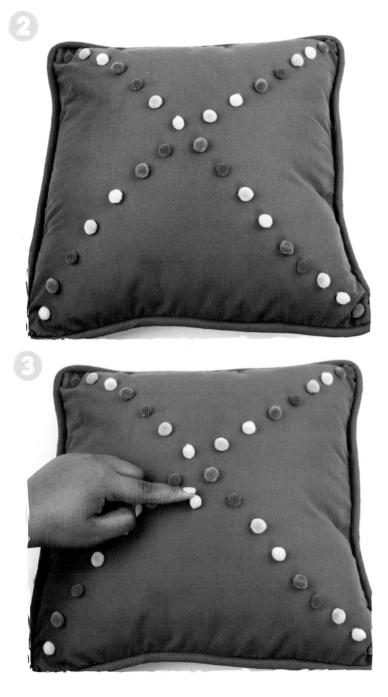

2 Continue adding pompoms to the front of the pillow from corner to corner in an X shape.

3 Now begin filling in the rest of the pillow with pompoms, working in diagonal lines. If you are using multicolored pompoms, try to stick with a pattern of alternating colors. The most important part of this step is gluing down the pompoms in straight lines.

4 Now wait for your creation to dry, which should take about 15 minutes. This pillow will be delicate, so remember to remove it from your bed before sleeping. If pompoms fall off, you can easily glue them back on.

GOLD PILLOWCASE

If I told you that a luxe Gold Pillowcase could be made with just an inexpensive bundle of fabric and a glue gun, would you believe it? Well, believe it or not, that's all it takes to make this awesome pillow! Pick any fabric you want and make a fold here, place some glue there, and bada bing, you have an amazing throw pillow to decorate your bed. Sounds pretty easy, right?

materials

- Pillow form (18" × 18" recommended)
- Stretchy gold fabric (48" × 48" recommended)
- Ruler
- Scissors
- Glue gun

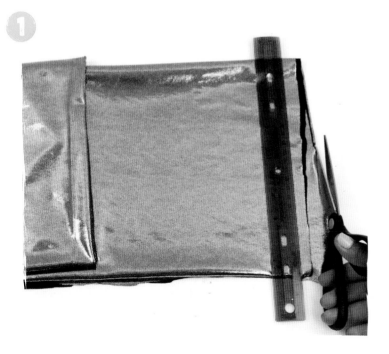

1 The first thing you need to do is cut your fabric to the correct size for your pillow form. You can use any size pillow form you like for this project; just be sure to measure it correctly. The form I used for this project is 18" × 18", so I cut my fabric to be 48" × 48" so that I had 6" extra on every side when it was folded. That left me with enough fabric to cover the entire pillow plus extra for making the seams. I decided to use a 48" × 48" because when folded in half it gave me fabric the length of the pillow form with an extra 6". The exact measurements aren't the most important part, just as long as the fabric

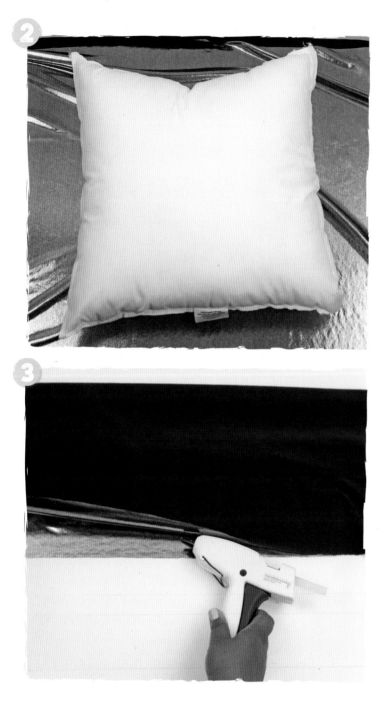

fits around the pillow comfortably with extra fabric for folding in.

2 Once the fabric is cut, double-check your fabric size by laying your fabric down on a flat surface with the gold side facing up. Place your pillow form to one side of the fabric, then fold one end of the fabric over the top of the pillow to the other end. Just by folding, you create one seam of the pillowcase. Turn the pillow in order to position the seam down at the bottom of the case, with the three sides remaining open.

3 Once you are sure the pillow form fits, remove it while keeping the fabric folded. The gold side of the fabric should remain on the inside for this step. With the seam at the bottom, carefully fold the edge of the upper layer of fabric up and run the glue up the two sides adjacent to the folded seam. Remember, you will be gluing gold side of the fabric to the gold. Press the two edges together. At this point you will be left with a pouch with an open end. Don't glue the top opening shut!

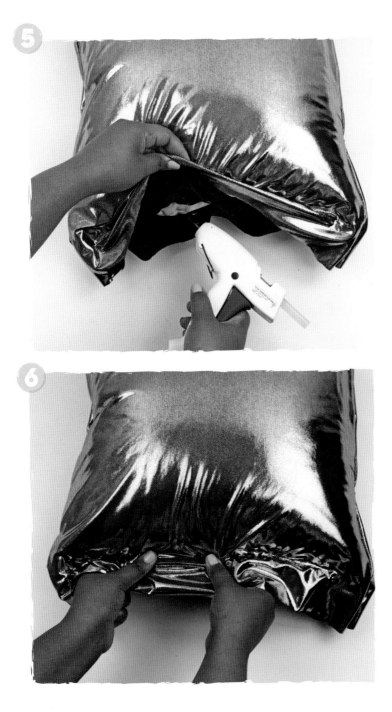

4 After the glue has a few seconds to dry, slide the pouch over the pillow to test whether you have made the pouch snug enough. If your pillowcase is too floppy, cut the glued portion off one side and follow the same process to glue the new seam shut. Once the fabric pouch fits snugly around the pillow form, flip the fabric pouch right side out again so the gold is showing.

5 Slide the pillow form in through the open end and close off the opening by adding glue near where the pillow ends. Place the glue in this step on the inside (mine was black) side of the fabric, gluing black to black.

6 Next, close off the opening by pinching the fabric together.

7 Cut off any extra fabric that is left over where you just glued. Try to make this cut as clean as possible, since it will be on the outside of the pillow. Wait about 5 minutes for the glue to fully dry, then it will be ready to use. When using the pillow, position this seam down so that no one can see it.

SEQUIN CURTAIN

This '90s-inspired DIY Sequin Curtain will bring the ultimate bling to your window or wall. When the light hits the oversized sequins it will bounce all around your room for a cool disco-ball effect that will make your friends so jealous they'll want to make one, too! It's the ultimate item to have for a party, or to add some whimsy and wonder to your room.

materials ✦●●●●●●●

- Fishing line (at least 100 yards)
- Scissors
- 3' dowel
- 320 (40-millimeter) sequins
- Glue gun
- Stick-on hooks (optional)

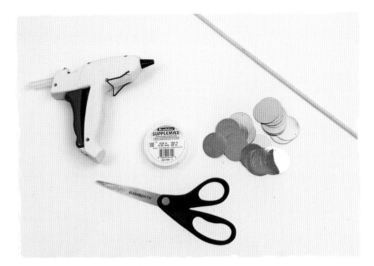

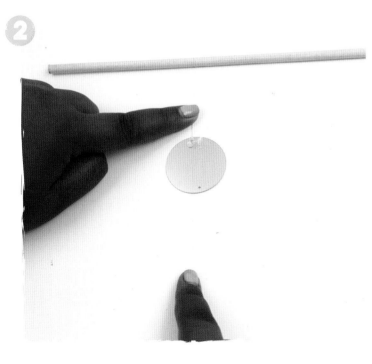

1 Start by using your scissors to cut the first strand of fishing line. How long the strand of fishing line is will determine how long your curtain will be. My strands were each about 40" long, and I cut 10 of them. It is always best to cut the strands longer at first, so that you can trim it to the size you want later. Once your line is cut, tie the first strand of fishing line to your dowel.

2 Now, place a sequin behind the fishing line up near the dowel. Use your glue gun to add a drop of glue to bind the line to the sequin.

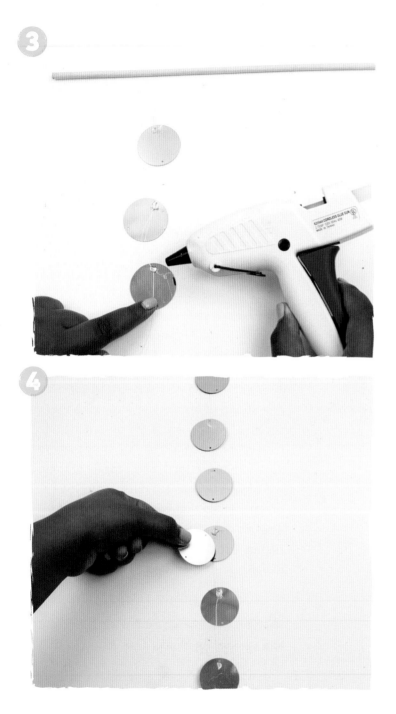

3 Before the glue is dry, place another sequin on top of the one you used in the previous step, sandwiching the fishing line in between.

4 Randomly space the sequins out along the line using the same gluing method, working downward until you are satisfied with the number of sequins. In total, I used about 16 pairs of sequins on each line.

5 Repeat these steps to complete as many sequin strands as you need along the dowel, so that the sequins of the neighboring line are just touching but not overlapping. The amount of sequin strands you need will be based on your dowel length; I used 10 strands to complete the curtain shown in the photos.

6 After you have finished all of the sequin strands, hang the rod in a doorway, over a window, or just on the wall with stick-on hooks for a fluttery, sparkly look.

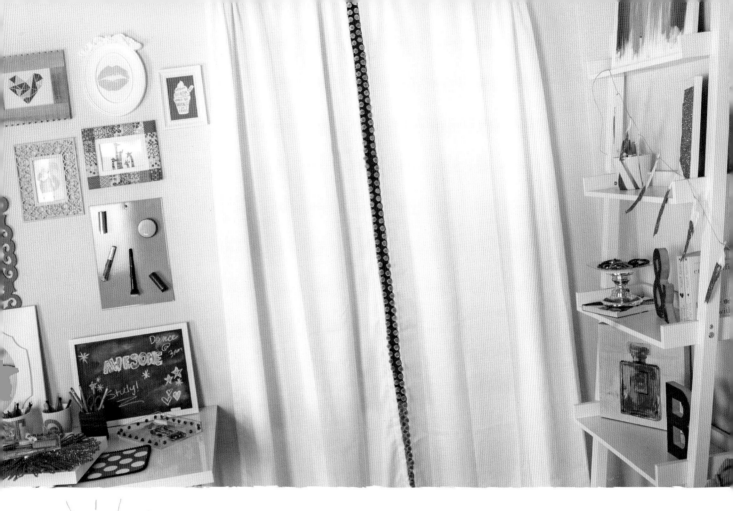

POMPOM CURTAINS

You can add pompoms to just about anything—see the Pompom Pillow project earlier in this chapter!—but my favorite way is to add them as trim to a curtain. These super-cute Pompom Curtains make a perfect frame for the light coming through your windows and into your room. Choose from an assortment of colors for your pompoms to match the rest of your DIY décor. You can even coordinate them with your bedding for a look that is store-bought!

materials

- 2 (84") white curtain panels
- 5 yards pompom string
- Glue gun
- Scissors

1 Start by laying your first curtain out on a flat surface, with the front of the curtain facing downwards. The reverse side of the curtain (the part that usually is against the window) should be facing up.

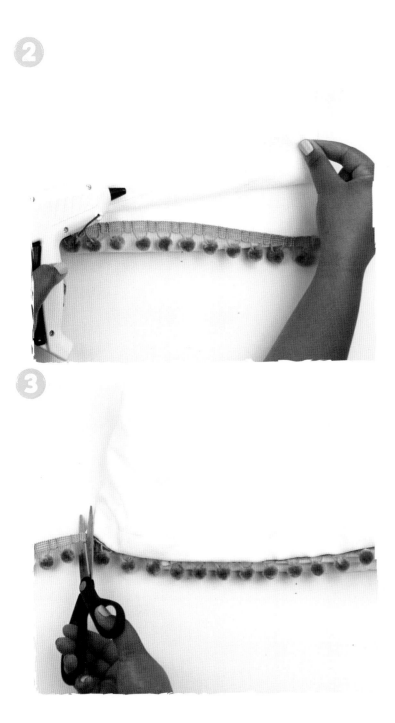

2 Starting at the top of the curtain, begin gluing down the pompom string to the inside edge, so that when you hang the two curtains up, the pompoms on the edge of each curtain will face each other. Be careful not to glue the loop at the top of the curtain shut, because this will still need to be open when you string the curtain onto the curtain rod.

3 Once the pompom string is glued all the way down to the bottom of the curtain, cut off the extra.

4 Repeat the same steps for your second curtain. If your curtains have a definite front and back, make sure that you are gluing the pompom strings to the *back* of the curtain so that the pompoms, not the string, will both face outward and toward each other.

5 Wait 10 minutes for the curtains to dry. When both curtains are done, slide them back on to your curtain rod to hang them in your window.

DIP-DYE CURTAINS

Let's be honest, store-bought curtains are never exactly the way you want them. So why not make your own and get exactly what you want, while saving money in the process? All you need are some plain white curtains, some dye, and a little bit of time. Once you master the simple technique that you'll learn here, you'll find yourself dip-dyeing everything you own!

materials

- Pink Rit dye (either liquid or powder will work fine)
- Large glass bowl
- Newspaper or cardboard (optional)
- Rubber gloves (optional)
- 2 (84") white polyester curtain panels

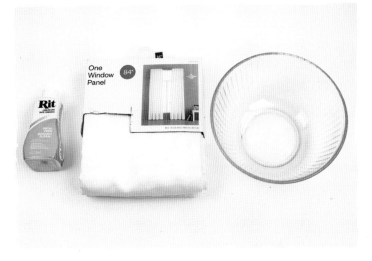

1 Mix your dye in a bowl according to package instructions. If you are worried about the dye staining your hands or the floor, lay down some newspaper or cardboard under your workspace and use rubber gloves when handling the dye or curtain.

2 Next, submerge the entire curtain in the dye to give the curtain its base color. Leave the curtain in the mixture until the fabric becomes visibly colored, about 5 minutes. To achieve this effect, stir the curtain around in the dye gently but constantly.

3 Then put the dyed curtain in the washing machine on the lowest cycle in cold water without any soap. When you remove the curtain from the washing machine, the result should be a pale pink hue. After you remove the curtains from the washing machine, run the washer once through with nothing in it to remove any traces of the dye that may have been left in the machine.

4 While the curtain is still damp from the washer, dip the bottom quarter of the curtain back into the dye and leave overnight.

5 The next day, lightly rinse only the bottom dip-dyed portion under warm running water. Hang the curtain to dry.

6 Follow the same steps to complete your second curtain, and you are good to go! If your curtains are a bit wrinkly, you can go over them quickly with a warm iron as needed.

Make It Personal!

Many dyes suggest using cotton fabric, but polyester works well for this because it doesn't soak up the color as well, which helps to get a pale pink. Not a pink fan? That's okay! Choose any color dye like blue, green, or a combination to personalize your funky new curtains.

CH6 LIGHTS, LANTERNS, AND LAMPSHADES

It's time to light up your room in ways you never thought possible! This chapter is all about making your room glow with some quick modifications to your lighting, so get ready to turn those typically boring lights into artsy and unique pieces that can stand on their own as room décor! Whether you're glamming up a table lamp with a Ruffle Lampshade, transforming string lights into Ping-Pong Ball Lights, or using cupcake liners to make an everyday lantern extraordinary, this chapter will help you spruce up your existing, boring lighting with options that will make your room shine! You will want your lights to be front and center after these upgrades!

PING-PONG BALL LIGHTS

Looking for a new twist on standard string lights? Look no further! Trust me on this one; adding Ping-Pong balls to ordinary, everyday strand lights gives them an awesome update that's sure to steal the show. These Ping-Pong Ball Lights are an inexpensive alternative to traditional round lights, and can be made in minutes! These will sure look awesome strung around your head-board or just above your bed for a cozy, warm, lighted effect.

materials

- 35+ Ping-Pong balls
- Ballpoint pen
- 1 strand string lights

1 To start, you need to make a hole in your Ping-Pong ball that is large enough for a single light to fit through. Do this by positioning the pen where you want to make a hole in the ball. If your ball has a logo that you don't want to show, this is the best place for the hole. Slowly and carefully twist the pen into the ball using slight pressure. This will ensure that your pen doesn't split the ball or go all the way through the other side.

2 Push one light from your string through the hole in the ball so that the ball covers both the bulb and the plastic socket.

3 Repeat this process until all of the lights have been covered by a Ping-Pong ball, then hang the lights on your wall!

Make It Personal!

Make your lights stand out by using colored Ping-Pong balls, or keep it classy with white! Either way, the lighting in your room is going to look great!

CUPCAKE LINER LANTERN

You probably love cupcakes, but did you know that you can use the liners for more than just baking? It's true! All you have to do to amp up a lamp or any other flat, boring room accessory that could use some extra color is add cupcake liners. This liners used on this on-trend lantern not only create a unique and flashy décor piece but also allow the light to shine through to give your room the magical ambiance you deserve.

materials

- 80 standard-sized cupcake liners
- Glue gun
- White paper lantern light with stand

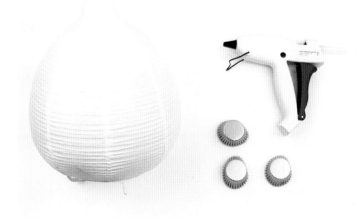

1 Gently turn your cupcake liners inside out. Don't worry if they get a bit wrinkled, it just adds to the effect!

2 ❷ Use your glue gun to add glue to the outside of the flat bottom of the cupcake liner before putting it on the lantern.

3 Glue the liners to the lantern, starting at the top. Make sure to place them close enough together so that you cannot see any white from the lantern peeking through.

4 Once you cover the whole lantern with liners, wait 10 minutes for it to dry, plug it in, and enjoy!

Make It Personal!

Check out Ikea when looking for your lantern light; they have several that could work for this project!

RUFFLE LAMPSHADE

Tired of your flat, boring lampshade? Try adding some ruffled ribbon to yours for an easy, instant upgrade. This project is way cheaper than going out and buying a fancy lampshade, and you get to play with ruffle fabric! It's a win-win! This is one of the tamer DIY projects in terms of bright colors and intricate patterns, but it will definitely give your lamp a more interesting look that complements your desk or nightstand décor. Being on trend is all about the little details, and having a cool lampshade completes the picture!

materials

- Lampshade
- 3 yards ruffle ribbon or fabric
- Scissors
- Glue gun

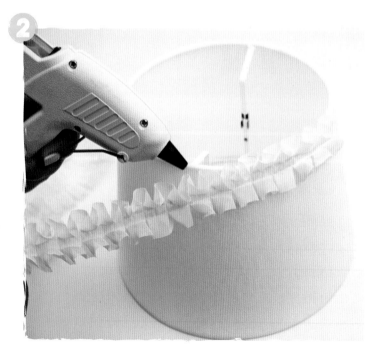

1 Take your lampshade and wrap your ruffle ribbon around it as many times as necessary to cover it, to determine how much you will need. Trim the ruffle ribbon, leaving a couple of inches more than you need, in case of any errors.

2 Once you have the length of ruffle ribbon correct, use your glue gun to glue one end of the ribbon to the lampshade.

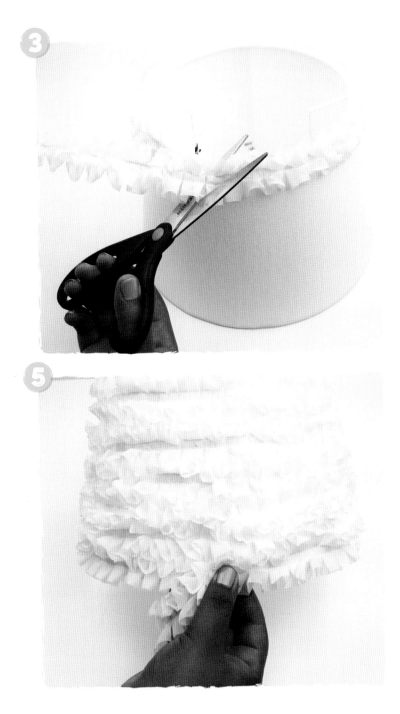

3 Working from the top down, go around the lampshade one time with the ruffle ribbon, applying glue as you go to secure it down. Once you get back around to the start of the ruffle, cut it off to create the first row.

4 Just beneath the spot where you started the first row, glue another row of ruffle ribbon around the lamp, and cut the ribbon once you get back to the start again.

5 Keep adding ruffles the same way until the lampshade is covered all the way down. Wait 10 minutes for the glue to dry, and you're ready to put it on the lamp, plug it in, and admire your work!

RIBBON CHANDELIER

This project is so much fun because you get to do the best kind of shopping . . . ribbon shopping! With all of the different types of ribbon available, you'll feel like a kid in a candy store when you get into the ribbon aisle in the craft store. You can pick out super-fun colors and styles of ribbon that match your room décor or your personality, or ones that you just can't stop looking at. The Ribbon Chandelier makes your room so frilly and girly that it's an absolutely perfect project if you're looking to make a statement. You can use twine to attach this Ribbon Chandelier to a pendant light if you have one in your room, or pop it over a plain lampshade for a totally great look!

materials

- 5–7 rolls of assorted ribbon in a variety of widths
- Scissors
- 7" embroidery hoop
- 30" twine, cut into 3 (10") pieces
- Ceiling hook (optional)

1 Cut the ribbon to lengths between 12" and 36". The length is up to you; you can vary each one or make them all the same.

2 Loosen the embroidery hoop all the way, but don't separate the inner and outer pieces.

3 Feed the ribbon between the two hoops, pulling each ribbon about three-quarters of the way through. Continue until you've used all of your ribbons.

4 Once you get all of the ribbons into the hoop, move them around so that they're evenly distributed around the entire outer hoop. Try to get all of the pieces close together, but avoid overlapping.

5 Now that all of the ribbon is positioned how you want it, tighten the hoops a bit and gently pull the ribbons through so that there is only about 1/2" looped through the hoop, with the rest hanging over the outer edge.

6 Once all of the ribbon is in place, tighten the hoops the rest of the way so the ribbons are secure.

7 To hang up this chandelier, tie the three 10"-long strands of twine around the embroidery hoop, equally distanced from each other. Bring the three strands of twine together and attach them to your ceiling over an existing pendant light or hang on a ceiling hook, if desired.

LIGHTED FLORAL PEACE SIGN

Unleash your inner flower child with this rad way to light up your room! This Lighted Floral Peace Sign is perfect if you're over the basic string light look since it adds light to your room in a totally unique way. Wrapped in a vine of your favorite floral, this DIY décor is sure to be the envy of all of your friends. Plug this baby in, and it's time to peace out, girl scout.

materials

- 18" grapevine wreath
- 6' faux flowers on a vine
- 1 strand string lights (battery-powered string lights recommended)
- 30" flower lace
- Scissors
- Glue gun

1 Begin by laying out your wreath and wrapping the vine of faux flowers around it. Intertwine the faux flowers with the branches of the wreath by lacing it through the nooks and crannies. Secure the ends of the vine by tucking them into the wreath so they are hidden.

2 If you're using a battery-powered strand of lights, secure the battery pack by situating it in a section of faux vine on the back of the wreath. Then start stringing the lights around the wreath by tucking various sections through the branches of the wreath. Since most

battery-powered light strings are fairly short, you'll want to keep the entire string in the front of the wreath. It is easiest to use wire string lights, since they are flexible but keep their shape, so it is easy to bend them around the branches.

3 Measure and cut a length of the flower lace going from the center top of the wreath to the center bottom.

4 Measure and cut two identical shorter portions of flower lace, going from one-third up the first piece of lace down on a diagonal to the edges of the wreath. These two pieces of lace should complete the peace sign.

5 Use your glue gun to glue the long piece of flower lace to the top and bottom of the wreath. Then, glue the two shorter sections of flower lace to the long piece in the middle, then glue the remaining ends to the edges of the wreath to form the peace sign.

6 Allow 10 minutes of drying time, and your lighted floral wreath is ready to hang!

Make It Personal!

If you can find them, battery-powered lights work best for this project. If you can't, don't worry; you will just be limited to keeping this near an outlet.

CH7

HOLIDAY DÉCOR

Want to create some holiday cheer? Then gather up a few of your friends, make some hot chocolate, and brighten up your room with festive and fun holiday décor projects! When the snow is on the ground, holiday crafts are so much fun to do with family and friends, whether you want to make them for each other or make them for yourselves, and you will have a blast creating and decorating everything in your room for the holidays. That's the best part, right? So hang your mistletoe—along with these super-fun DIY projects—and get ready for a very happy holiday!

BUTTON REINDEER SILHOUETTE

Let Rudolph guide the sleigh to your room for the holidays with this reindeer silhouette made out of buttons! This is such a fun way to add a cute animal design to your room for the holidays, and you won't want to take it down once they're over. Use your own extra buttons, or pick up some unique ones to make this project your own. You can use this method for a whole bunch of different things for any holiday. Consider making a button heart for Valentine's Day, or a gold button leaf for fall, or give your reindeer a Christmas tree friend!

materials

- Reindeer silhouette print from Google
- Stencil paper
- Pencil
- About 100 assorted buttons
- Glue gun
- Scissors
- 20" ribbon
- Frame (large enough to hold reindeer silhouette)

1 Start by tracing the reindeer silhouette onto the stencil paper. It's okay if it does not match exactly; the buttons do not allow the shape to be kept perfect anyway!

2 Glue buttons onto the stencil paper, keeping within the lines that you traced. It's okay to overlap the buttons a bit if it helps you keep a clearer outline of the reindeer.

3 Once you have filled in the outline of the reindeer with buttons, use your scissors to cut the extra stencil paper away.

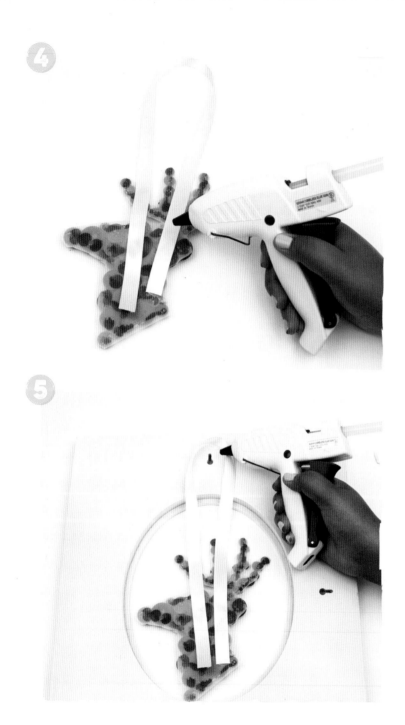

4 Turn the stencil paper over and glue one end of the ribbon to the reindeer head. Then create a loop in the ribbon and glue down the other end next to the first.

5 Turn your frame over and glue the top of the ribbon to the upper portion of the frame so that the reindeer hangs in the middle. If your frame has glass, remove it before hanging the reindeer.

6 Now hang your reindeer silhouette on the wall to celebrate your holiday spirit!

"LET IT SNOW" SHADOW BOX

When the weather outside is just a little bit too chilly, snuggle up inside and make this holiday craft. Use "Let It Snow," as seen in the photos, or pick a quote that reminds you of everything you love about the holidays. Even if there is not an inch of snow on the ground where you live, this "Let It Snow" Shadow Box guarantees that you will be feeling the winter spirit in no time—without all of the shoveling!

materials

- 1 (11" × 11") shadow box frame
- 1 sheet winter/holiday-themed scrapbook paper
- Scissors
- 1 small bag fake snow powder
- Ruler (optional)
- Letter stickers (roughly 4")

1 Turn the frame over so the glass is facing down. Remove the backing and insert from the shadow box, then use the insert to measure and cut your scrapbook paper to the correct size for the frame.

Make It Personal!

Choose any quote you want to personalize this project, but before you begin crafting make sure that your chosen quote will fit on the glass face of the shadow box. "Let It Snow" fit well on the 11″ × 11″ frame used in the photos.

2 Add fake snow into the shadow box so the frame is filled up around one-third of the way. Make sure not to spill, since fake snow can get messy! You want to add enough to create a layer of snow that will sit at the bottom of the shadow box once you stand it up. I filled one-third of the frame with snow for the perfect look.

3 Add the scrapbook paper and fasten the backing for the frame on to secure the snow inside.

4 Place the shadow box face up on the table and begin sticking the stickers to the glass top of the frame. If desired, use a ruler to create a straight edge as you place the stickers onto the shadow box to make sure they line up evenly. I overlapped my stickers on the word "snow," but you can just use smaller letters if you don't like the overlapped look.

5 When all of your stickers are placed in the correct order for your quote, you are done! Enjoy your new craft for the holidays!

CLIPBOARD HANGER QUOTE

You probably have an old clipboard lying around the house that you never use. The project teaches you how to turn that boring office staple into something uniquely spectacular. And all you have to do to freshen up this old standby is add a holiday quote and a bit of sparkly scrapbook paper. How easy is that?

materials

- Clipboard
- 1 sheet winter/holiday-themed scrapbook paper, 12" × 12" or 8" × 10" (8" × 10" preferred)
- Rotary cutter
- Quote printed on 8" × 10" paper

1 First, cut your scrapbook paper on either side so that it is about the same width as the clipboard. To make a clean line, use a rotary cutter to make all cuts. If possible, choose a paper that is 8" × 10" like notebook paper, so you don't have to make any cuts. Then insert the scrapbook paper into the clip at the top of the clipboard.

2 Cut your quote page using the rotary cutter, taking about an inch off each side so that the scrapbook paper will be visible when the cut-out quote is placed on top.

3 Insert your quote into the clip over the scrapbook paper, and the project is complete! Hang it on your wall or prop it up on your desk to add some holiday spirit to your space!

Make It Personal!

The best part about this project is that you can switch out the quote or the paper whenever you want. Just scan through Tumblr, Pinterest, and Google for an awesome quote for this DIY project, or better yet, create a saying of your own in a text document on the computer and print it out on 8" × 10" paper. Before you print, make sure the quote is positioned on the page with enough space on either side to cut off an inch from the edges of the paper. This will allow the scrapbook paper to peek out from behind. Then add scrapbook paper featuring fresh floral prints or fall leaves. Switching things up means you can use this all year round!

VASE WITH POMPOM BRANCHES

This DIY brings the outside in, which is perfect if you want to feel like a woodland fairy lives in your room! Simply adding pompoms to some fake branches adds whimsy and fun to any décor, but it's even better when you use it to enhance an already awesome DIY bedroom. This project looks great during the holidays because the pompoms look like pretty lights strung on the branches, a perfect alternative to buying fairy lights.

materials

- 4–6 branches
- Glue gun
- 40–60 (½") pompoms
- Vase

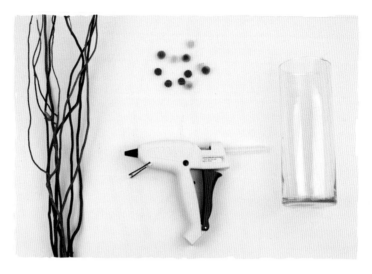

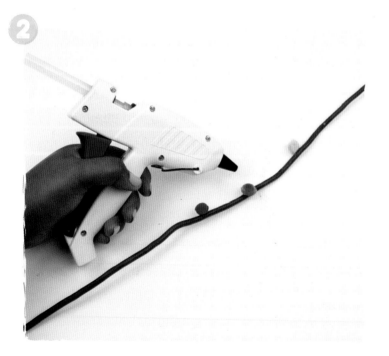

1 Take a single branch, and use your glue gun to add a small drop of glue to it, starting a few inches from the bottom of the branch. Then press a single pompom onto the drop of glue and hold it for a second or two until it adheres.

2 Continue adding pompoms along the branch. Concentrate the pompoms on the upper part of the branches that will be sticking out from the vase. You do not want to add too many, or your project can end up looking a bit too busy. I ended up using about 10 pompoms per branch.

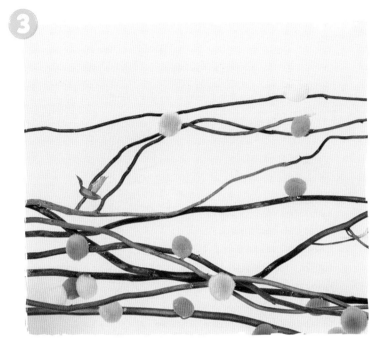

3 Repeat for the remaining branches, setting each one aside as you finish to let the glue dry.

4 Once all of the branches are dry (about 5 minutes), place them in the vase. Display this project somewhere in your room where the branches will be out of the way, as they can break easily.

. . . .

Make It Personal!

You can find sticks in the floral section of the craft store, or just grab a few from outside. Long, skinny branches work best for this project! Before you start this project, you may have to break your branches so they fit in your vase. Start by breaking off less than you think, and measure them against the vase until you get the size you like. You want most of the branches to be peeking out of the vase.

. . . .

INDEX

ABOUT THE AUTHOR

Tana Smith is the creator of the popular fashion and lifestyle YouTube channel *TanaMontana100*. She was bitten by the creative bug when she was challenged with decorating her drab college dorm room. Now, she loves creating fun, inexpensive DIY projects that liven up any space. This is her first book.